NEEDLEPOINT BY DESIGN

NEEDLEPOINT

ALL DESIGNS BY THE AUTHOR

BY DESIGN

Variations on Chinese Themes

MAGGIE LANE

CHARLES SCRIBNER'S SONS New York

13 15 17 19   MD/C   20 18 16 14 12
1 3 5 7 9 11 13 15 17 19   V/P   20 18 16 14 12 10 8 6 4 2

PRINTED IN THE UNITED STATES OF AMERICA

SBN: 684-10338-9 (cloth)
SBN: 684-173158 (pbk)

Library of Congress Catalog Card Number 71-123842

To RANDY

ACKNOWLEDGMENTS

I am grateful to my husband and my friends for their early and continuing appreciation of my work and for their encouragement.

To Jane Montant and Christopher Chodoff for getting me started, and to Elinor Parker, for editing this book, I give my special thanks.

CONTENTS

THE DESIGNS

FOREWORD

During most of recorded history, the spinning, weaving, embroidery, lace-making, knitting, needlepoint—all the many and intricate skills associated with the craft of fabric making—was woman's appointed work. With the coming of the industrial revolution, factory machines took over almost all of these skills. The ancient feminine monopoly of the crafts is hardly remembered today, save as we sometimes humorously refer to the "Distaff Side," to denote the female side of a family.

Nevertheless, needlework as a hobby, has survived the onslaught of the machine. Needlepoint, especially, is having a tremendous revival. This may be because, in the average home, where almost every object is mass-produced, a lovely handcrafted piece of needlepoint comes as a joyful relief to the eyes. (Many needlepointers seem to find, not only aesthetic pleasure in doing the work, but therapeutic benefits, claiming that nothing is better to relax the "up-tightness" we feel in our mechanized age, so full of conflicts and tensions.) In any event, "the media is the message." And a charming piece of needlepoint says to everyone who sees it, this house is lived in by a woman who is a creative personality.

Needlecraft is not an art. What "Art" is, is famously hard to define. But whatever Art is, Art is *not* utilitarian. A craft is primarily utilitarian. It is the making of something to be used by man. A craft, which is the more or less exact repetition of multitudinous actions, or skills, can also be taught to another person—any other person—providing that other has the required manual dexterity.

ix

Nevertheless, the needlepointer can also be something of an artist. She becomes an artist precisely when she creates her own designs, and selects her own colors and materials.

Let us take that very ubiquitous and useful article, a pillow. So far as its utility goes, a pillow designed and executed in needlepoint by Maggie Lane is no more or less comfortable to lean against than a pillow covered with ticking. I am the proud possessor of a number of pillows done by Maggie Lane. I have always been amazed and amused to watch my guests' reaction to them. As they go to sit down, they glance at them briefly, seldom making a comment. But somehow, something more than 'pillow' seems to have registered on them. For very often, while they are talking, they pull them out from behind their backs, lay them on their laps, stroke them, peer at them closely, and either begin to talk about them, or just plain sit back and enjoy them. That part of Maggie Lane's work which so delights the senses *is* Art.

I have many friends who have done vast quantities of needlepoint. Most of these women handle their needles expertly. But not all of them, regrettably, produce work that merits the endless hours spent on them. Too often the designs look as though they had been traced from rather tasteless Victorian wall paper, crude French tapestries, or even from children's picture books. Worst of all, are those little rugs and chair seats, covered with garish flowers, whose names would be unrecognizable even to the most sympathetic botanist.

What is the explanation for the existence of so much commonplace and poorly-executed needlepoint? Generally, their makers have bought "ready-made" designs, sloppily painted on canvas, together with the wool, which are sold today, by the big commercial shops, in vast numbers. (In a sense, these women are merely doing piece-work at home, on mass-produced objects.)

But why are they content to do so? I think it is largely because most women honestly don't know how even to begin to make their own designs, or how to pick their own colors. They do not realize that it takes only a little longer to do a perfect and precise rendition on canvas of an original design, than it does to do a careless and amateurish-looking one.

Maggie Lane's book is, I think, a modern "breakthrough"

book in the technique of the ancient, joyful, and beautiful craft of needlepoint. Her graph method, if patiently and faithfully followed, will insure precisely-executed design. It is, if one can use the word, scientific—every inch of the work is counted out on the canvas. And this, of course, makes everything come out beautifully even.

Her contribution to the *art* of needlepoint is also in the direction of simplicity. For she insists, again and again, on a good basic design (preferably original) and a limited "palette" of a very few well-chosen "personal" colors. This combination of precision, simple design, and limited color, explains the cool magic of her needlepoint.

One dares to hope that Maggie Lane's book will fall into the hands of the many women of taste who secretly yearn to do needlepoint, but who "can't stand all those cheap, gaudy, and complicated things you find in the shops." Such women, taking this book in hand, will be able to make needlepoint things of contemporary beauty that will become, in time, not only cherished family heirlooms, but collector's items.

CLARE BOOTHE LUCE

May 21, 1970

PREFACE

Needlework is one of mankind's oldest arts. It is mentioned not only in Exodus in the Bible but it has also been found in the tombs of Egypt dating back to the 15th century B.C. In spite of its antiquity, however, the art of needlepoint did not come into its own until the 12th century in China. The advent of machinery, however, caused a decline in the art until this century when it began to enjoy a revival.

Throughout this book you will note an Oriental flavor in my designs. My love for Chinese patterns is no accident. I was born of missionary parents living in the Orient, and spent my childhood years in China. When I was sixteen, the tensions of war impelled most American families living in China to leave the Orient for the United States. My parents packed in haste, leaving many possessions behind. We sailed into the safe harbor of San Francisco only a few months before the Japanese bombed Pearl Harbor.

The pace of American life, very different from life in China, kept me totally occupied for several years. I finished high school, majored in art in college, and had little time for nostalgia. It was only when I came to live in New York that I suffered my first pangs of homesickness. Then, what had begun as a vague wish to live again amid things Chinese soon became an obsession. But it was not until I married Myles J. Lane, now a justice of the New York State Supreme Court, that I could begin to satisfy my thirst for Orientalia.

About three years ago I realized I was spending more time

on a hobby than I spent at my easel, where for many years I had been painting professionally. I decided then to get the hobby out of my system once and for all. I closed my studio and began making needlepoint pillows in a Chinese style. It was at this time that I began working on the series of designs contained in this book.

In the January 1969 isue of GOURMET there appeared a color photograph in which three of my pillows were featured. Since then I have received more than one hundred and fifty letters asking me where my designs could be bought. It is for this reason that I now want to make available to you my portfolio of designs for needlework. The drawings, on graph paper, include a variety of central motifs and as many border patterns. Each design was first conceived as a small Chinese rug, and many of the borders are, in fact, drawn from borders appearing on ancient Oriental rugs.

It is my hope that my 20th century search for serenity, lost to me for a time when I first left the old country to come and live in this new, mechanized world, may, in some way, benefit you in the hours you spend with these designs inspired by the ancient art of the Orient.

MAGGIE LANE

New York, 1969

NEEDLEPOINT BY DESIGN

Introduction

In many ways working needlepoint from a graph has been most rewarding for me. Once I have started a canvas I find it difficult to stop. Because I seldom color a graph I do not know what the finished design will look like when worked in the colors I have selected. So I push on until I have worked an area large enough so that the design begins to reveal the secret of its ultimate character. This is usually so tantalizing that I work far longer than I should. It has frequently been said to me that it must take the patience of Job to do the kind of work I do. My answer is always that it takes impatience. You see, it is hard to wait for the moment when the last stitch has been worked and I finally hold the finished pillow in my hands. The excitement I feel then is my reward and is worth the many hours of work and impatience.

Many of the persons to whom I have taught my method of doing needlepoint have told me that they too have worked long hours, even far into the night, because of an intense desire to see how the design will look after they have done "just this one bit more." The person working on a painted canvas derives no such thrill from the drama unfolding before the

3

eyes. For them the design exists from the beginning and they need only to cover it with wool.

Each person I have taught has also described to me the pleasure felt when the complexities of the design were at last worked out on the canvas. Their sense of accomplishment was akin to that experienced after the solving of a difficult puzzle.

An interesting story comes to mind about a woman living in New York who bought several of my designs. She worked them in many different ways. Her daughters, who were also needleworkers, then borrowed the designs from their mother and began to work on them.

One of the daughters came with her husband one day to spend a week with her mother. At that time both mother and daughter were working on extremely complicated designs.

One evening after dinner the three sat talking. When, after a while, the son-in-law said he was going to retire, the daughter said she would follow later but that now she wanted to "have a little chat with Mother."

The older woman, suddenly concerned, began to imagine that some trouble must be brewing between her daughter and son-in-law. As soon as he left the room the daughter perched on the edge of the sofa beside her mother who braced herself for the news. Some tense moments passed before the girl finally blurted out: "Look, Mother, I'll show you where I made a mistake in my work if you'll show me where you made one in yours!"

This book is written primarily for the beginner, who has never worked needlepoint on a painted canvas. It is also for the accomplished needleworker who is willing to try something more challenging than covering a painted pattern.

This is a teaching book. In it I shall show you, step by step, how to do needlework from a design worked out on graph paper. Symmetry and precision of detail are best achieved by this method and perfection is the result.

Turn to the back of the book where you will find a series of designs in graph form. You will also see illustrations showing many of these designs as finished works.

Although the book deals mainly with pillows, the method and the designs can be used to make many other things. We shall consider them later.

Each design, like a small Chinese rug, has a central motif and a border. If you particularly like one border but prefer the central motif shown with a different border you are free to follow your own taste. All the central motifs in the square designs will combine well with any of the squared borders. You therefore have a wide variety of combinations from which to make a selection.

When you have decided which border and which central motif you wish to use, two more basic decisions must be made before you can actually begin your needlework. Both decisions further affect the way the pillows will look because they determine the choice of yarns for your work.

TONAL VALUE

With few exceptions the patterns are designed to be worked in three tones, light, medium and dark.

Black and white mark the outer limits in tonal value. There is nothing darker than black nor lighter than white. When the two are used together they generate more visual excitement than two shades of gray used together. Also, when a light pattern is used against a dark background it looks more dramatic than the reverse. So, if drama and excitement are what you want in your pillow, choose a dark tone for the background and a light tone for the pattern. If, however, you want a more subdued effect, chose a more medium tone for the background and a medium light, rather than white, for the pattern. The closer the tonal value the greater the loss of contrast, therefore the greater the loss of drama and excitement, and the more subtle the effect.

COLOR

When selecting the colors for your pillow I would suggest that you first consider the colors in the room, the most important one being that of the sofa or chair where you plan to place your finished pillow. I do hope you do not intend to put it on a sofa or chair upholstered in printed fabric. Design upon design is sometimes very effective, but I believe that these designs look best against plain fabrics.

I planned most of the designs for one basic color which is generally used for the background. The central motif and the border pattern is usually worked in white or off-white, with only one accent color for added interest. The pillows were planned this way because I believe in using restraint when it comes to the number of colors woven together in a small area. In an 18″ square the use of too many colors could result in chaos. I design with beauty and serenity in mind.

If your sofa or chair is medium blue, for example, the rug beige, the walls off-white and the accent color grass-green, I offer the following schemes for your pillow:

1. Off-white and beige for the central motif and border.
    Bitter grass-green for the accent color in central motif and
    in border.
    The blue of your sofa or chair as the background color.

2. Light blue, same color as sofa but lighter tone, for the cen-
    tral motif and border.
    Dark blue, perhaps toward navy, for accent color in central
    motif and border.
    The blue of your sofa or chair as the background color.
    This is known as a monochromatic combination, meaning
    that a single color is used, tonal contrast alone providing
    the interest.

3. Medium and dark blue for the central motif.
    Bitter grass-green for the accent color in central motif and
    border.
    Beige or off-white for background color.

4. Off-white and beige for central motif and border.
    Dark blue or navy for accent color.
    Bitter grass-green for background color.

For a general discussion of Color, see page 32.

 # Materials

Before you can proceed further you will need the following items:

CANVAS

In most needlework stores two types of needlepoint canvas are available. They are *penelope* canvas and *mono* canvas.

PENELOPE CANVAS is a double thread canvas. The intersections of the double threads are woven together. This locks the intersections. The canvas is therefore good for the half-cross stitch. But since we shall not be working the half-cross stitch we shall not be using penelope canvas.

MONO CANVAS is a single thread canvas that looks like screening except that it is woven with linen or Italian hemp threads rather than with wire. It comes in white and also in an unbleached form. (I prefer the latter because it keeps its crispness longer.) *Mono canvas is best suited to our needs* because the holes in the canvas, i.e., the spaces between the warp and woof threads, are larger than those on penelope canvas. Working on mono canvas is therefore less tiring to the eyes than working on penelope canvas.

Mono canvas comes in several weights. That is, the mesh, or the intersections of the evenly spaced warp and woof threads, ranges from 10 to the running inch up to 40 to the inch. This latter weight is actually a fine gauze and we need not consider it. Canvas with 12 threads to the inch, which I shall call #12 canvas, is the mesh for which I designed, and on which I made my pillows.

When you work, each stitch will cover one intersection of the warp and woof threads of the canvas. So on #12 canvas you will work 12 stitches to the running inch, or 144 stitches to the square inch.

NOTE: If you want to make your pillow larger or smaller than the size indicated on the graph use a different weight of canvas. For a larger pillow use #10 canvas and for a smaller one use #14 or even #16 canvas, depending on how small you want your pillow to be. The way to estimate the size of the finished pillow follows: if the graph measures 201 small box-stitches in width and 201 small box-stitches in height, divide 201 by the number of threads to the inch on the canvas you intend to use. #10 canvas will make a pillow about 20″ square, #12 canvas will make a pillow about 17″ square, #14 a pillow about 14½″ square, and #16 about 13″ square. There is always a small difference between the exact size you figure your pillow will measure and the size of the outline you will draw after counting off the canvas threads. This is due to slight irregularities in the spacing of the threads.

Good canvas is made of firm fibers of even thickness. It is sized to keep it crisp and fresh while you work on it. The sizing also keeps the intersections of the threads in place. The more highly polished the threads the better the canvas. The unbleached canvas of which I spoke earlier has threads more highly polished than those of bleached, white mono canvas.

When you select canvas, look for a piece that has no flaws, like knots or uneven threads in it. You want no weakness in the material on which you are going to spend your precious time and effort.

Buy a piece of canvas large enough to allow for a 3″ margin on all sides around the area you plan to cover with needlework. Since most of the designs were created for pillows which would measure 17″–18″ square when worked on #12 canvas you will need the following sizes of canvas depending on the weight of canvas you select:

26″ square for #10 canvas
24″ square for #12 canvas
21″ square for #14 canvas
19″ square for #16 canvas

Binding the Raw Edges of Your Canvas. Use masking tape 1″ wide, or fabric binding sewn on by hand or machine. I use the masking tape. It serves the purpose for which it was intended, namely, to keep the edges of the canvas from raveling as you work. It is quickly and easily applied. I am usually so anxious to get to the actual needlework that I bless all short cuts that serve me well.

NEEDLES

Buy Boye tapestry needles, #18 for #12 canvas.

THIMBLE

Use one. I live in mine.

SCISSORS

Use a pair of small, sharp-pointed ones.

WOOLS

There are several types of wool you can use for needlepoint. Knitting and crocheting wools are not among them. They will not do because they have short, fluffy fibers and therefore are not strong. Needlepoint wools must have the strength of long fibers, for you will be pulling each thread many times through the canvas. Select your wools from the following types:

CREWEL WOOL is a springy two-ply yarn that can be used on #12 canvas, two threads covering it very well.

PERSIAN WOOL comes in a very wide range of colors and has a 3-strand thread which is readily separated into single strands. Use 2 strands to cover #12 canvas.

TAPESTRY WOOL is a well-twisted yarn that covers #12 canvas perfectly just as it comes from the hank.

OTHER YARNS

SILK. The floss comes from France. It is more expensive than wool. It comes in nine yard skeins. If you want to use it for a change of texture, use all the 7 threads that cling together as you take them from the skein. You may experience some difficulty in working with silk. It is hard to run the needle through the back of your silk when you want to anchor a new thread, and frequently one of the single threads among the several with which you are working will turn stubborn and make a loop on the surface of your work. Then you will have to stop and pull your thumb-nail along the threads as yet unworked. This often snags and pulls the loop out of the worked stitch.

COTTON. Use D.M.C. cotton. It comes in a good range of colors, each well shaded from light to dark. Use the group of threads that adhere together, thread them through the needle and use them double for #12 canvas. (You may have the same trouble with cotton as you have with silk. See above for solution.)

SILVER AND GOLD THREAD. This beautiful thread comes from France. "Au Cabas D'Or" is the brand to buy. Cut a piece of thread no longer than three feet in length. Thread one end through the needle, then use the thread double. Drag the two lengths of the thread several times over a piece of beeswax. The thread will then lose its annoying tendency to twist and curl. Don't worry about the wax on the thread. It can easily be removed. When you have finished working the metallic stitches, place your work face down on an absorbent surface. Cover the back of the canvas with a clean cotton cloth. Press the work with a warm iron. This will remove the wax.

FRAMES

You will NOT need a frame for your work. The stitches you will be using are all stitches that require a single thrust of the needle into and out of the canvas. If you were to stretch your canvas on a frame it would become taut. You would then have to use two motions for each stitch. One hand would have to be in front of the canvas to insert the needle, the other hand behind the canvas to return the needle to the front of the canvas again, a slower process than the single in and out thrust mentioned above.

Heavy lines both directions ≈ 1" (ie first thread in box)

A small motif which can be used alone or in combination with others

 # Stitches

For your work you will need two basic flat stitches, and three bump, or lump, stitches.

FLAT STITCHES

CONTINENTAL STITCH. This basic stitch is for outlining areas in the central motif that you will fill in later with the basket-weave stitch. It is also used wherever a single line of stitching is needed.

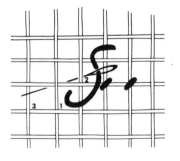

THE CONTINENTAL STITCH

BASKET-WEAVE STITCH. This stitch is for background work and all filling wherever there is more than a single

14

5 tones are used in this design:

1. Light   – yellow
2. Medium light – blue
3. Medium   – brown
4. Medium dark   – blk-brown
5. Dark   – bright brown (hairy)

1. #5 – black areas
2. #1 – white on beetle bk
3. #3 – hind legs, head, shoulder, antennae
4. #4 – dotted areas
5. #2 – fill in blue-grad – outline the curved ends before filling in blue

line of stitching needed. The basket-weave pulls the canvas askew less than any other simple background stitch. In addition you can work your stitches without having to turn your canvas around all the time. For these reasons I recommend it.

THE BASKET-WEAVE STITCH, going up the canvas or from right to left

THE BASKET-WEAVE STITCH, going down the canvas or from left to right

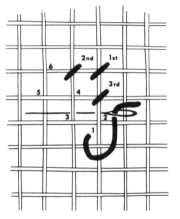

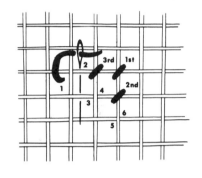

NOTE: All flat stitches should be worked to slant in the same direction, i.e., each stitch should look like a grain of rice tilted from upper right to lower left.

Special Note About Working the Basket-Weave: Never work two rows of basket-weave in the same direction. If you do, a diagonal line will show faintly on the surface of your work. Also, when casting off the ends of your threads, and running in the new threads you want to anchor preparatory to working, do it in random directions. If you follow a directional pattern casting off and running in, it will also show faintly as a directional pattern on the surface of your work.

You can tell where you should begin your next row by looking at the back of your work. If the threads of the just completed row run horizontally on the back of your canvas (see illustration) you must start at the upper left hand side on the front of the canvas. If the threads of the just completed row run vertically on the back of your canvas (see illustration) you must start at the lower right hand side on the front of the canvas.

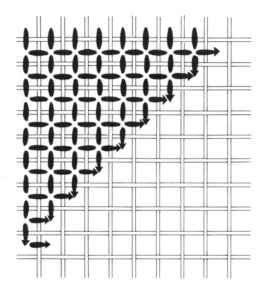

WORKING WITH THE CANVAS GRAIN

I made a discovery during the years spent working on mono canvas. *Canvas has a grain* with which it is best to work. I do not know whether or not anyone else has noticed this fact. No one, to my knowledge, has ever written a word about it.

While working with black wool on white canvas I observed one day that through part of my needlework the canvas threads were faintly visible here and there under the black stitches. On the part of the work just finished, however, the wool covered the canvas completely. I turned the canvas over and looked at the back of it. I had made the mistake of working two rows in the same direction! Looking again at the front of the canvas I saw the division line between the well-covering stitches and the others lay along the line where I had worked the two rows in the same direction. I wanted to work so that the stitches would always cover the canvas as completely as possible so I examined the relationship between my stitches and the weaving of the canvas. This is what I saw:

When I work from lower right to upper left, I ply my needle parallel with the horizontal canvas threads as they appear coming out of the worked stitches. The needle should go in and come out between horizontal threads humping OVER vertical threads.

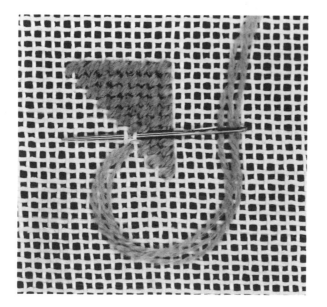

RIGHT WAY

When I work from upper left to lower right I ply my needle parallel with the vertical canvas threads. The needle should go in and come out between vertical threads humping OVER horizontal threads. (SEE ILLUSTRATION.)

Working with the Grain helps you to know in which direction the next row should go even before you turn the canvas to look at the back. It should help to keep you from working two rows in the same direction.

When worked wrong, as in illustration below, the needle is going in and coming out at right angles to the direction of the canvas threads coming from the worked stitches.

See also, 182 in Charleston

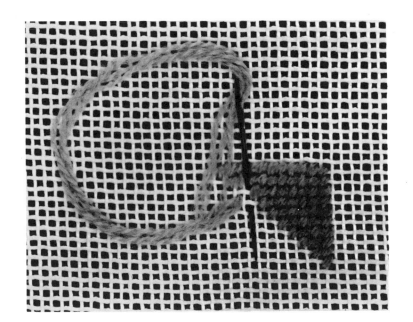

WRONG WAY

BUMP STITCHES

SMYRNA CROSS STITCH. This is a bump stitch worked over two horizontal and two vertical threads.

SMYRNA CROSS STITCH

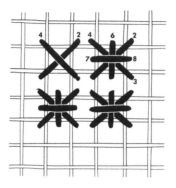

DOUBLE LEVIATHAN STITCH. This is a bump stitch worked over four horizontal and four vertical threads.

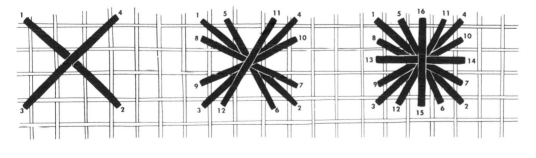

DOUBLE LEVIATHAN STITCH

TRIPLE CROSS STITCH. This is a bump stitch worked over three horizontal and three vertical threads. It is for use in the center of patterns which have an uneven number of stitches in their width and length, thus having a center axis.

TRIPLE CROSS STITCH

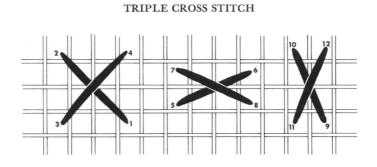

NOTE: All bump stitches should be finished with the final thread running from top to bottom, with the exception of the triple-cross. Its final thread has to run from upper right of center to lower left of center.

Starting to Work

You now have in front of you the following: a piece of bound canvas, wool, needles, a thimble, and a pair of scissors. You know the kind of design you are going to make, what colors you will use in the work and you know how large your pillow will be when it is finished. You know how to make two basic flat stitches and three raised bump stitches. You wonder, now, how you are going to transfer the design from the graph to the canvas. The answer is that you will do it by reading from the graph as you work. This is like reading notes of music on a page and playing the notes with your fingers on an instrument. Here I quote from the book *Oriental Rugs in Colour* by Preben Liebetrau, page 17. He is talking about rugs made in the East. "Here the weaving is directed by a *salim,* as he is called, who recites or monotonously intones the design being copied. Or again, the design may first be set down in colour on squared paper, each square indicating a knot. The weaver follows this coloured chart much as the pianist follows his sheet-music.

"Beautiful results are obtained only through exact and careful workmanship."

MARKING THE CANVAS

Fold the canvas in half, then in half again. In this way you will find the center of your canvas.

MARK THE HORIZONTAL AND VERTICAL CENTERS OF YOUR CANVAS. Use a nylon-tipped marking pen. Draw a dotted line ALONG the horizontal and vertical threads radiating from the center of your canvas. Do this only if there is an UNEVEN number of box-stitches on the graph you plan to follow. (SEE ILLUSTRATION.) Where there is an EVEN number of box-stitches on the graph draw the dotted lines for the horizontal and vertical centers BETWEEN two canvas threads.

OUTLINE THE AREA TO BE WORKED. On the graph, count off the number of box-stitches from the center lines out to the corners. If the whole graph measures 201 x 201 box-stitches, count off 100 canvas threads to the right and to the left of the vertical center of your canvas. Count off 100 canvas threads above and below the horizontal center of your canvas. Then draw the outlines around the area just counted. The outlines should enclose an area containing 201 threads across and 201 threads from top to bottom. NOTE: when drawing the outline do not draw the line ALONG a thread but BETWEEN the 100th thread and the 101st.

MARK GRAPH LINES ON CANVAS. An X marks the center box-stitch on your graph. This is where there is an uneven number of stitches to the graph. An X also marks the center of your canvas where the two center lines intersect.

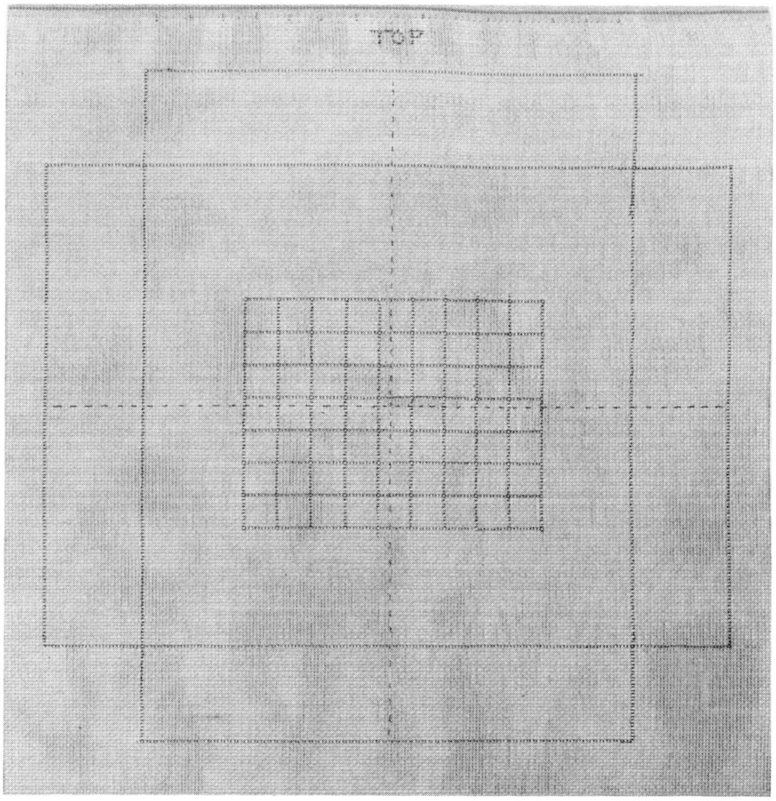

(⁜ marks the center of each graph with an even number of box-stitches.)

Each graph is made up of a cross-hatch of fine lines. Each of the resulting small squares represents a stitch. I have been calling them, and will continue to call them, BOX-STITCHES.

Every tenth line on the graph is a heavier, darker line. These lines outline squares containing 100 box-stitches. Duplicate these heavy lines on your canvas. The purpose of drawing these lines on the canvas is to create a frame of reference that corresponds to the grid of heavy lines on the graph. This will reduce the possibility of error in counting your stitches. (The squares you outline on your canvas will be filled with 100 stitches.)

IMPORTANT: Each box-stitch on the graph represents a crossing of a horizontal and a vertical canvas thread, or the stitch which will cover it, *not the hole between threads*. Conversely, each crossing of threads on the canvas corresponds to a box-stitch on the graph.

MARK THE TOP OF YOUR CANVAS WITH THE WORD "TOP."

MARK THE FIRST GRAPH LINE. Use a blue drawing pencil. (*Prismacolor* is good. Do not use regular lead pencil on canvas. It always grays the wool.) If on your graph three box-stitches separate the first heavy line ABOVE the center from the center box-stitch (with an X in it) count off three canvas threads ABOVE the horizontal center thread, then draw a horizontal line BETWEEN that third thread and the fourth. Similarly, if four box-stitches on your graph separate the first heavy line to the RIGHT from the center box-stitch (with the X) count off four canvas threads to the RIGHT of the vertical center thread, then draw a vertical line BETWEEN that fourth thread and the fifth. (SEE ILLUSTRATION.)

Now draw horizontal lines to separate rows of 10 horizontal threads, and vertical lines to separate rows of 10 vertical threads. Use the first 2 grid lines you drew as the lines from which you count off your rows of 10.

When you have finished you will have a canvas covered with a grid of blue lines corresponding to those on the graph. This will make it easy to do *Needlepoint by the Numbers*. NOTE: if the lines drawn on the canvas come off on your wool, don't worry. Wait until the field is finished, then sponge it with a clean cloth and cleaning fluid.

Let us finally begin needlework.

Working and Finishing

Specific instructions for each central motif and border start on page 37.

When I work I sit on a sofa with a light to my left. I place my graph to my right and use my small sewing scissors as a pointer to indicate, on the graph, the area from which I am reading at the moment. I do so from the beginning to the end of the "fancy work." After I have finished all the difficult pattern work I put away the graph. Then I can relax and enjoy filling in the background.

So thread your needle with the color you need to start your central motif. Place your scissors on the graph, points toward the first box-stitch you will make. Let us say this stitch is in the first square below the square containing the center box-stitch (with the X in it). Find the corresponding square on the canvas. Let us say that the first box-stitch, on the graph, is the third from the right side of the square, and the fourth up from the bottom side. On your canvas find the corresponding crossing of threads, and you are ready to make your first stitch.

Run your needle in basting stitches across 3″—4″ of

canvas until the point is next to the spot where you will make the first stitch. Make it, and you are on your way.

Follow the direction of box-stitches shown on the graph as you make your next stitches, and also count the number as you work. The heavy lines on the graph and the corresponding lines drawn on your canvas will help you in this respect, i.e., counting. Continue working until you have finished your first length of yarn. Then run the needle and yarn through 8—10 stitches on the under side of your work. Disengage the tail of the yarn you left at the beginning of work and thread it through the eye of the needle. Run it also through 8—10 stitches on the under side of your work. *Always clip off excess yarn* each time you finish a thread. Otherwise you will catch the ends of loose threads hanging from the back of your canvas. These threads may come through to the front of your work, and if they do they will prove very disturbing and annoying.

Re-thread your needle, run it through 8—10 stitches at the back of your work to anchor the tail end, then continue with your work.

When working develop an even rhythm. Never pull the thread hard. Instead, put the needle into and out of the canvas and then pull it, in a single motion, only until the yarn lies flat in the stitch. Roll the needle slightly, your thumb moving against your forefinger, *away* from the tip of the forefinger, toward the first knuckle joint. This will help to keep the thread from twisting.

BLOCKING THE CANVAS

DO NOT WET THE CANVAS. It is not necessary if you have used the basket-weave stitch. And wetting the canvas might cause the running of any ink lines drawn on it. Instead, block with a steam iron and damp or wet cloth. Place the cloth over the canvas and, while ironing, pull the canvas *hard* against the direction in which it has warped. Don't be afraid of it, it won't tear. Then pull from the sides, then from the top and bottom while the canvas is still hot and steamy. Correct the corners and press dry.

FINISHING TOUCHES

After I have steamed and blocked the canvas and before I cut off the excess canvas, to leave 8—10 threads outside the worked area, I use a sewing machine, set at 12 stitches to the inch, and stitch a zigzag or wavy row or two of stitching between the finished needlework and the seventh or eighth thread *away* from the finished needlework. Then when I cut the canvas it won't ravel.

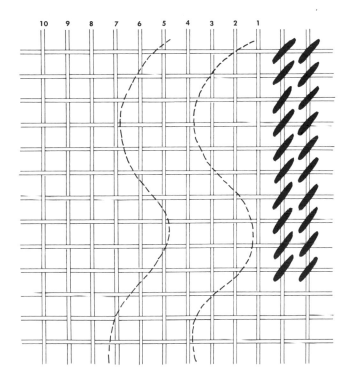

SEWING FABRIC BACK
TO NEEDLEWORK

With the insides out, sew heavy silk fabric, matched as closely as possible to the background color, to the needlework. I pin the two together first, then sew with the machine. I sew the pieces together with the needlepoint piece on top so I can run my seam *between* the finished work and the next, uncovered canvas thread. Sew three sides of the square, and an inch or two on each side of the fourth side. Remove pins. Fold back the *fabric* flap on the unsewn side of the casing, press it so it will have a straight crease in it. Turn the casing right side out. From inside the casing push the corners out. Fill the casing with a custom-made pillow, 60-40 down and feathers. Pin the backing to the needlework on the unsewn side and slip-stitch the two together.

Although the pillows have been designed so they do not need a braid or welting, you may wish to add this finishing touch. I suggest you make a braid out of the same kind of yarn you used in the needlepoint.

Buy an uncut hank of the color of yarn you want. Unwind three lengths of wool about 6 or 7 yards long. Use a #7 Bates crochet hook and three strands and crochet a single chain-stitch braid long enough to edge the pillow. Sew the braid on the pillow after the casing has been filled with the inner pillow.

Before pinning the braid to the casing to cover the seam joining the needlework to the fabric backing, tuck in the loose threads at each end of the braid: thread them singly in your needlepoint needle and work them back into the braid. Then pin the braid to the pillow seam. NOTE: the flat side, that

which looks like a braid, is the underside. Slip-stitch the braid to the pillow cover along the back, then along the front of the braid, i.e., two times around the pillow.

Although the central motifs were designed with pillows in mind they can be adapted to many other uses. One lady made two squares—with the frog on one, the crab on the other —and sewed them together to create a very handsome tote bag, once she had added handles. She also used a circular floral motif on the top of a needlepoint cover for a typewriter. She worked the design in hot pinks and fern greens on a bone ground, and piped the seams with hot pink.

Piano benches, foot stools and chair seats can all be handsomely dressed in needlepoint using these designs.

If the project requires some figuring on your part you can make your own graph.

Buy one large sheet of 17″ x 22″ graph paper, or as many sheets as you will need. Buy the kind that has 100 box-stitches to the square inch. It is easy to count, and easy to read. It is the kind I use for designing.

If you want to make a piece of needlepoint 15″ square on #12 canvas, multiply 15 x 12. You will then outline a square on your graph 180 x 180 box-stitches. Work out your design within this area.

If you want to design your own central motif, outline the area that you wish it to fill on your graph. Rough it out on a separate sheet of paper, perfect the drawing, then trace it onto the graph paper. After this you must adapt it to the box-stitch lines of the graph paper, making the step-lines with which you are by now familiar, having seen them in all the graphs in this book.

You may color your graph if you like but do it lightly, otherwise you will obliterate the grid lines, making the graph difficult to read.

When your graph is finished proceed as directed in the instructions for making pillows.

If the area to be covered is irregular, such as that of a chair seat, take a piece of brown paper and make a pattern of the area. Cut off the excess, and outline the pattern on the canvas. Then find the center of the area on the canvas, mark off horizontal and vertical lines and the graph lines and proceed as directed in the pillow instructions.

When you make glasses cases, use #16 or #18 mesh. Finish the two pieces, block them and stitch the zigzag row of stitching around the needlepoint. Then cut off the excess canvas. Turn in the raw edges. Steam and press them. Catch the edges to the under side of the work. Take pellon and cut two pieces slightly smaller than the area of the finished pieces. Use "Sobo" to glue the pellon to the wrong side of the canvas. Take lining fabric—silk broad-cloth is excellent—and cut two pieces slightly larger than the case size. Turn in the raw edges and pin the two lining pieces to the undersides of the two pieces of needlepoint. Slip stitch the lining to the casings. If you like, you may pad each piece slightly with cotton or felt placed between the back of the needlepoint and the silk lining. Then place the two pieces of lined needlepoint together, right sides out. Use background-color wool and your needlepoint needle to whip the two pieces together. Make sure to stitch through every edge stitch in your work so the finished piece will be symmetrical when you have finished.

Steam and press again.

These central motifs and borders, originally having been conceived as small rugs, are uniquely suited for rug-making. Instead of using #12 canvas you can use #8 penelope canvas, or as it is sometimes known, #16. This is available in two widths, 36" and 60". It is the only canvas made in the 60" width. You can order it from "Boutique Margot, 26 West 54th Street, New York, New York 10019."

You can make 25" square rugs or plan larger rugs, making your own graphs following the instructions given in the previous chapter. When working on this #8 canvas use 4 strands of Persian yarn.

When you finish your rug it is best to have it blocked, sized, bound and lined by a professional.

Notes on Color

COLOR: "The quality in virtue of which objects present different appearances to the eye, in respect of the kind of light reflected from their surfaces." *The Oxford Universal Dictionary,* 1955.

What a dry description of a quality that has aroused emotions from the beginning of time! Red, white and blue, for instance, call up the feeling of loyalty to the flag. Blue alone can make us think of the sea or the sky, or of Monday's moods. Yellow represents either the sun or cowardice. Green stands for verdure or envy, and red can mean either roses or anger, etc.

There are three primary and three secondary colors. Red, yellow and blue are the primaries. A primary color IS and cannot be achieved by a mixture of colors. The secondary colors, orange, green and violet, are the results of the mixture of two primary colors; red and yellow make orange, yellow and blue make green, and blue and red make violet. We see the total range of colors in the rainbow: red, orange, yellow, green, blue and violet.

When you place the colors on a color wheel they read as follows, each color opposite to its complement:

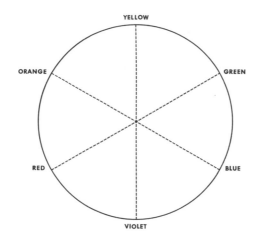

If you like you can slip the tertiary colors in the circle; red-orange goes between red and orange, orange-yellow between orange and yellow, yellow-green between yellow and green, and so forth.

Although you will not be mixing pigments to obtain the colors for your wools, the following information may prove helpful to you when you select the colors for your work.

When white is added to a color its tonal value is lightened. Its tonal value can be darkened by the addition of a dark neutral, such as brown, gray or black. (However, the chromatic value of the color will be slightly reduced by the addition of the dark neutral. The very word "neutral" should tell you the added darkener will neutralize somewhat.) When you place two different colors next to each other you can easily see which color is the lighter of the two by half-closing your eyes, or squinting, while looking at them. NEVER use together, side by side, two different colors of the same tonal value UNLESS you want visual vibrations.

Going further we learn that a pure color, red, for instance, injected with a drop of its complement, green, will become slightly less intense. The more of the complement we add to the original color the more it loses its brilliance until it finally reaches the absolutely neutral state when in our case it is half red and half green, and can no longer be called either red or green.

So now we know that color has three qualities: 1) its hue, i.e., red or yellow or blue; 2) its tonal value, i.e., its lightness or darkness; 3) its chromatic value, i.e., its brilliance, intensity or neutrality.

Colors, like notes on the piano, make music. Some seem to melt together and harmonize while others clash in a disagreeable and atonal way. But *there are no ugly colors*. For every color you think of as unattractive there exists a color or combination of two colors which, when placed beside your "ugly" color, makes it beautiful.

Take, for example, eggplant; not a particularly handsome color when seen by itself, but frame it with putty and robin's egg blue and you have a beautiful chord. Or maroon with turquoise and cream. Or greenish fawn with teal-blue. Some of the schemes I have used have come to my notice by accident. I have a camphor chest full of yarns and when I am ready to begin work on canvas I go to the coffer and pull out all the wool. Sometimes two or three skeins fall close together, the colors harmonizing so beautifully that I wonder why I never before thought of that combination. One such trio was a muted amethyst, cognac and a clay white.

When selecting your colors remember that the more muted the scheme, the more subtle must be your selection of the kind of white to use. The Persian yarns offer many shades of white from greenish through blue and neutral to a warm, rich cream.

Only when you plan to use black or a sharp, clear

Frog pillow, as shown on page 59.

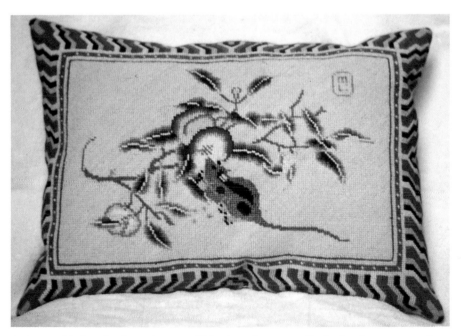

Mouse Eating Apricots design will be found on page 87, the border on page 48.

LEFT: zigzag glasses case, page 102.
RIGHT: beetle glasses case, page 104.

Serenity pillow worked in three colors; directions on page 79.

A Parsons table; directions are given on page 95.

Motif from the dragon rug (see color picture opposite page 66) made into a pillow, with the scallop pattern on page 104 used as background, set off by a simple border.

A rug which uses an extended version of the scenic pillow pictured on page 78; the border is diagrammed on page 85.

An envelope purse in petit point.

color for your main hue should you select pure white to use with it.

In *The Tiffany Studio Collection of Antique Chinese Rugs,* printed at Hillacre, Riverside, Connecticut, for the Tiffany Studios, 1908, there appears a short chapter on the colors that were employed by the Chinese rug weavers. The first paragraph points to the basic difference between Chinese rugs and those made in other parts of the eastern world. The observation is made that primary red never appears in Chinese rugs. Instead, the weavers used fruit colors such as apricot, persimmon, pomegranate and peach, all these colors being warmed with gold. In Persian rugs, on the other hand, reds of great brilliance and depth were used, many of them verging on cerise or magenta, both violet-reds. It is then pointed out that the Chinese limited themselves to a narrow palette, two or three colors, but four or five tones, i.e.; "two shades of yellow, two shades of blue, and one of cream"; or "two shades of blue, cream and apricot red." Other eastern rugmakers used a wide range of colors and tones, i.e.; "yellow, two shades of blue, cream, several shades of green, fire-color, turquoise-blue and many shades of red."

Here I would like to make an observation of my own on two additional qualities that make Chinese rugs unique:

1. The patterned areas are usually relieved by plain fields.

2. There is always a serene, well-scaled border, echoing the colors and tones used in the patterns in the field.

When a designer limits his range of color to two or three, he must offer something else to create interest in his design. Pattern is the answer, and pattern is created only by differences in tonal value.

I have noted here for you the characteristics of antique Chinese rugs because they set standards of excellence that were my guide and goal when I created the designs in this book.

Pillows using some of the motifs detailed on the following pages

Stag Beetle Pillow · 16¼″ x 16¼″

The pillow measures 195 threads by 195 threads. Bind off a piece of #12 canvas measuring 21″ square. Mark the center threads, outline the pillow, and mark the graph lines where you will work the stag beetle.

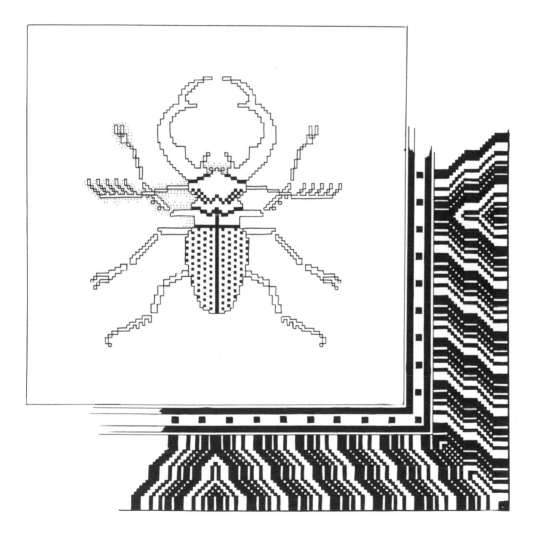

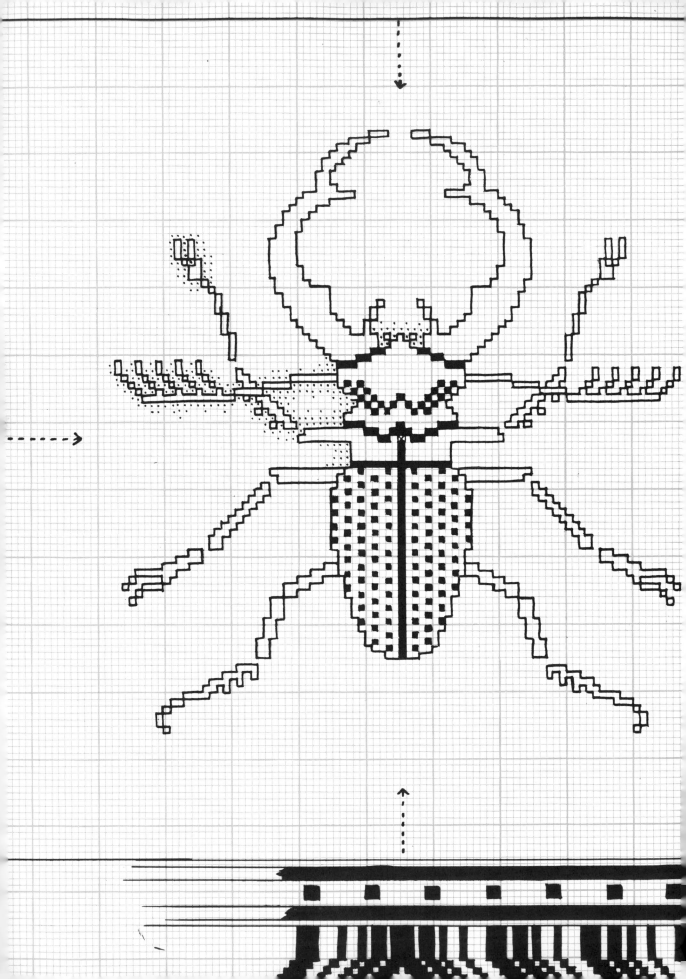

Only two tones are used in this design:
    #1 White, or light tone.
    #2 Black, or dark tone.

NOTE: At the top of the line marking the center of the beetle's back there is a single square, left white, then filled with an x. (Work it in dark tone when you come to it.) This box-stitch represents the center of the graph and corresponds to the center of your canvas. Use it for reference when you begin work.

1.   Using #2 tone, dark, work line up beetle's back. Then work all other stitches in beetle's body marked in black on the graph.

2.   Using #1 tone, light, outline beetle's body and antlers, then fill in. Work his two feelers and 6 legs. (If you use initials, work them in a medium tone accent color in the space outlined by the antlers.)

Directions for the border illustrated on page 37 follow on page 40, but you may substitute any of the other borders shown in the book.

3. Using #1 tone, light, outline the inner border, i.e., work the single lines at inner and outer edge of this dotted band.

4. Using #2 tone, dark, work Smyrna cross stitches in the inner border. These are the black squares marked on the graph. Then work the two double rows of black at either side of the band.

5. Using #1 tone, light, fill in background of band with black squares on it.

6. Using #2 tone, dark, work background of pillows, up to border just completed.

7. Using #1 and #2 tones, light and dark, work zigzag outer border.

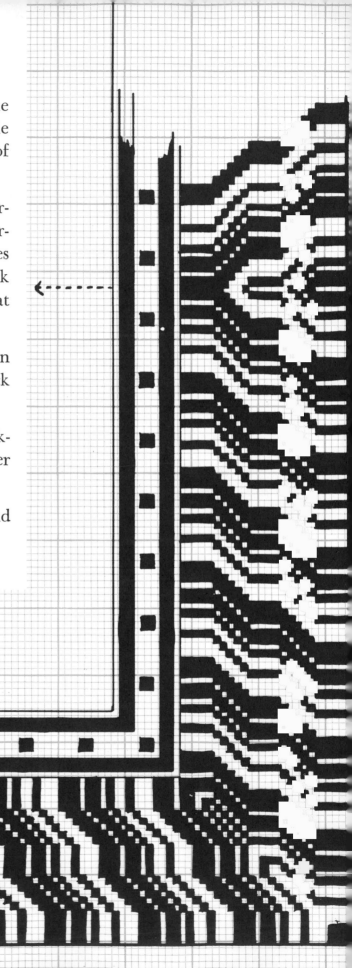

Turtle Pillow · 17" x 17"

The turtle pillow measures 202 threads by 202 threads. Bind off a piece of #12 canvas measuring 21" x 21". Mark two center lines, then outline pillow and draw graph lines in the area where you will work the turtle.

The following 4 tones and colors are suggested for the turtle pillow:

1. Light   White
2. Medium light   Light Beige
3. Medium tone   Amber
4. Medium dark or dark   Olive Green or Black

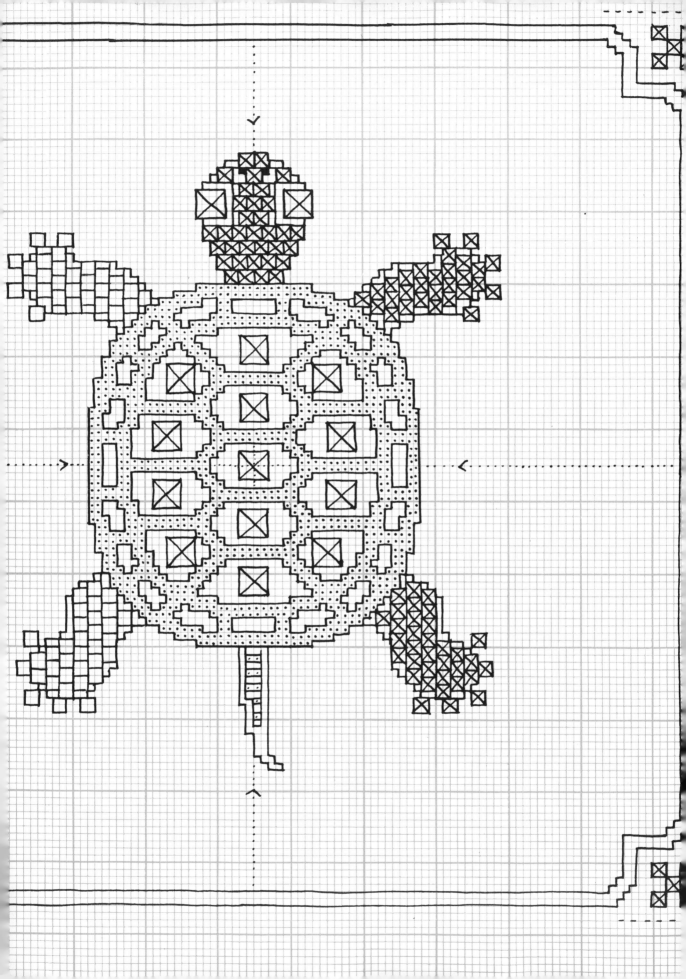

Dotted lines intersect in the middle of the double Leviathan stitch square in the center of the turtle's back. Where they cross marks the center of the graph and corresponds to the place on your canvas where the two center lines meet. Use this point for reference when you begin work.

1. Using #2 tone work outer outline of turtle's shell. Work inner outline of turtle's shell. Work separations between thirteen lozenges on turtle's shell. Work separations between inner and outer outlines of shell.

2. Using #1 tone work double Leviathan lumps in each of the thirteen lozenges. Fill in remainder of each lozenge and also white areas in frame of shell. Work outline of tail and white lines in tail, then using #2 tone, work dotted or shaded lines in tail.

3. Using #1 tone work head, up to eye level, in Smyrna cross-stitch. The stitches not crossed in head, arms and legs will be worked as regular, flat stitches. Using #2 tone work the outline around eyes. Using #3 tone work double Leviathan lumps for eyes. Finish head up to nostrils, working again in #1 tone. Using #4 tone work two nostrils, then finish head. Using #1 tone work Smyrna cross stitches in arms and legs, and fill in flat stitches in same tone. Work 5 Smyrna cross-stitches for fingernails and toenails on each appendage.

4. Using #2 tone work two row outline around field, i.e., the one with the in-turning corners.

5. Using #2 tone work 5 lumps in each corner, outside outline worked in step 4.

6. Using #1 tone work key fret border.

7. Using #4 tone work background within field border, then background to key fret border.

8. Using #2 tone work 6-line outer border.

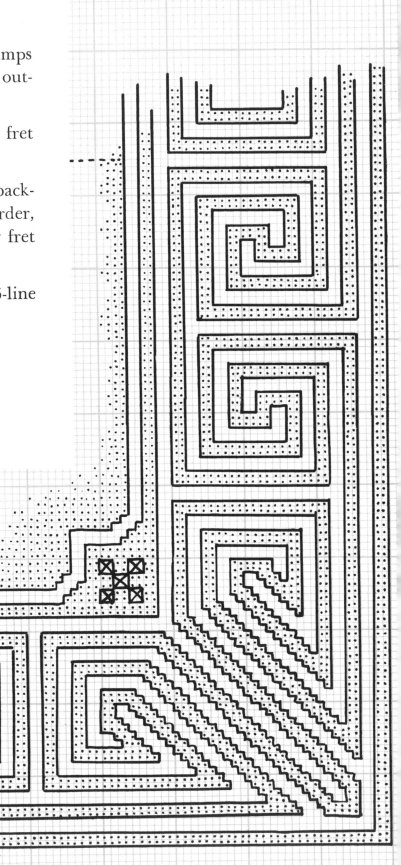

Baby Turtle Pillow · 13½″ x 13½″

The pillow measures 161 threads by 161 threads. Bind off a piece of #12 canvas measuring 18″ x 18″ square. Mark center threads, outline work area, and mark graph lines where you will work the baby turtle.

A black dot slightly off center in the turtle's back marks the center of the graph. It represents the crossing of the two center threads of your canvas. Use it for reference when you begin work.

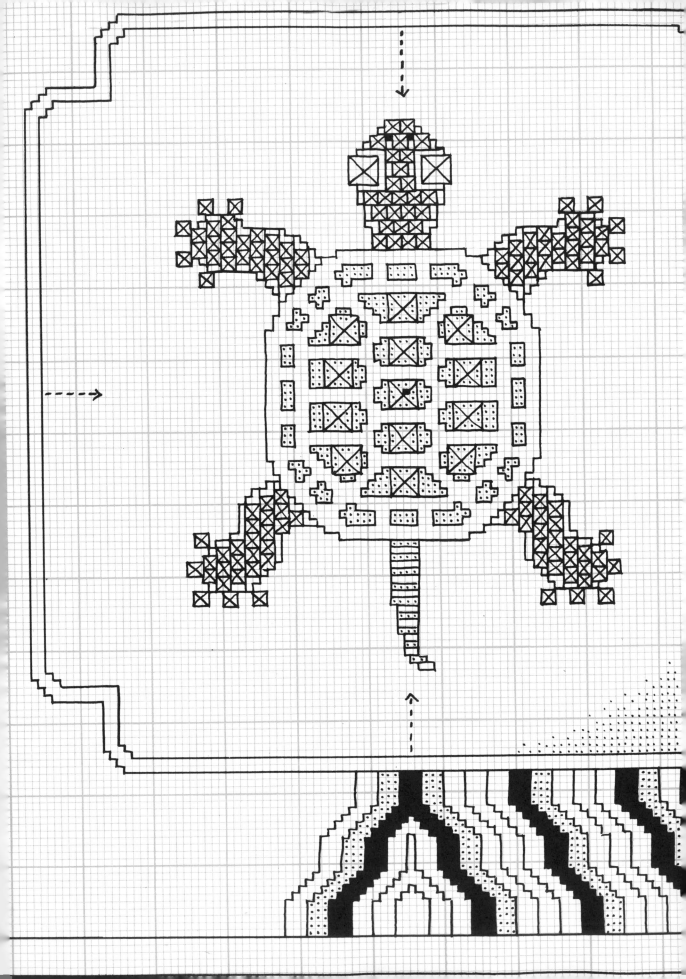

5 tones are used in this turtle pillow. I also suggest the following five colors:

1. Light   White
2. Medium light   Beige
3. Medium   Greenish Gray
4. Medium dark   Tobacco Brown
5. Dark   Black

1. Using #1 tone work unshaded portion of turtle's shell.

2. Using #3 tone work double Leviathan stitches in each of 13 lozenges in turtle's back, then fill in all dotted or shaded areas of his shell.

3. Using #2 tone work Smyrna cross-stitches for turtle's head, up to the eyes. Use #3 tone to outline eyes, and perhaps a brandy brown for the double Leviathan stitch eyes. Continue #2 tone Smyrna cross-stitch up to the #5 nostrils, then finish head.

4. Using #2 tone work turtle's arms and legs in Smyrna cross-stitch.

5. Using #3 tone work turtle's fingernails and toenails.

6. Using #2 and #3 tones work turtle's tail.

7. Using #1 tone work band around face of pillow, i.e., the in-turned corner band two stitches wide.

8. Optional: Using #3 tone work initials in dotted squares.

9. Using #5 tone fill in background around turtle.

10. Using tones #1 through #5, work zigzag border. Use #5 where it is black on the graph, then #4 for the dotted or shaded line, #3 for the next, #2 for the next, and #1 for the fifth line. Then the black line, #5, begins the shading again.

11. Using #1 tone work outer band, five stitches wide.

Fish Pillow, Boxed · 10" x 13⅓" x 2½"

The face of the pillow measures 120 threads x 160 threads. The flaps are 30 threads deep. Bind off a piece of #12 canvas measuring 19" x 22". Mark the outlines, including those for the flaps. Then mark the center lines and the graph lines where you will work the fish. *Do not mark graph lines in the corners until you are ready to work them.* The illustrated corner motif will be used for all four corners. You will turn the book each time you work a corner. Then, *and only then,* when the illustrated motif is turned in the proper way for the corner you plan to work, should you mark the helpful graph lines for that particular corner.

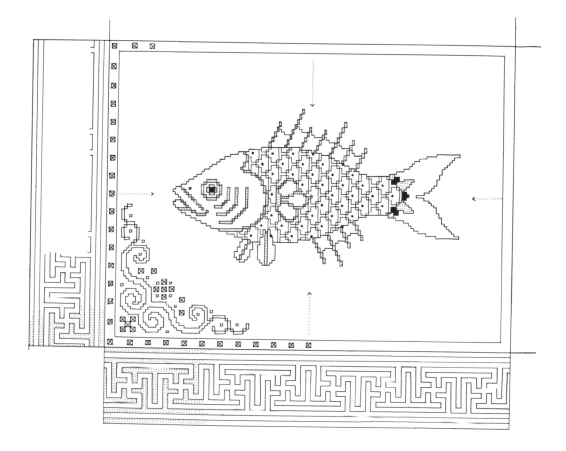

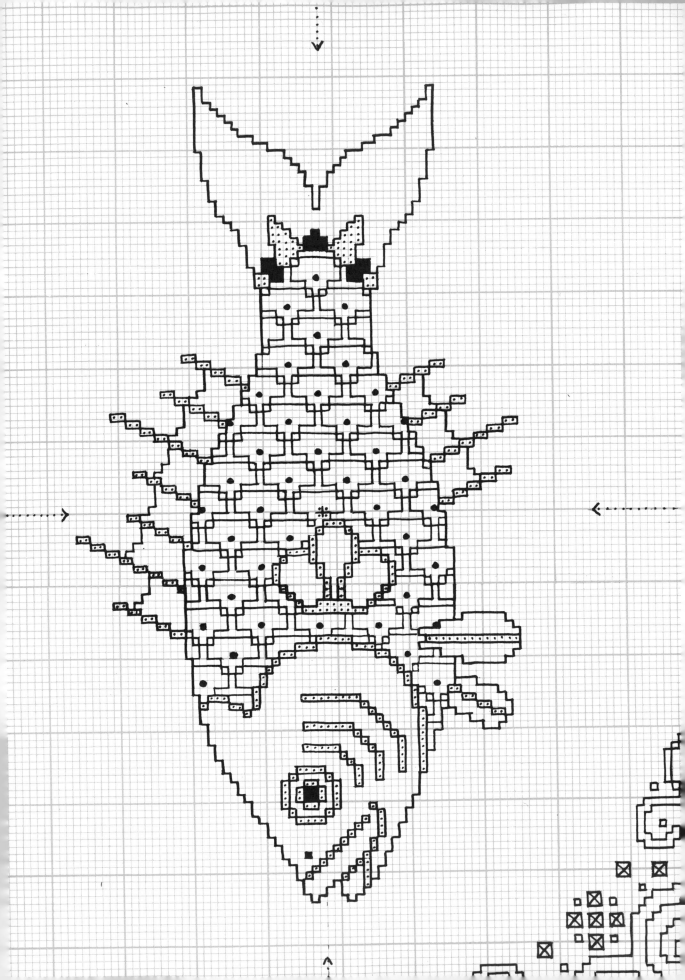

The following tones and colors are suggested for the fish pillow:

1. Light   Off-White
2. Medium light   Saffron Yellow
3. Medium   Burnt-Orange
4. Medium dark   Taupe or Gray
5. Dark   Black

✜ marks the center of the graph and indicates where the center lines drawn on the canvas intersect. Use this point for reference when you begin work.

1. Using #4 tone outline the head, work the three lines behind the eye, the outlines of the mouth and the eye. Then work the dotted lines in the two forward under-fins, the three-lobed fin in the body, and the spines on the upper and lower fins.

2. Using #5 tone work black iris in the eye, and the dot for the nostril.

3. Using #3 tone work shaded ring around pupil of eye.

4. Using #2 tone work unshaded ring in eye.

5. Using #1 tone outline head, then fill in. Then outline and fill in lower, forward fins and fill in fin in body.

6. Using #1 tone outline each scale.

7. Using #5, tone, dot each scale, as shown by black mark on graph.

8. Using #2 tone, fill in scales.

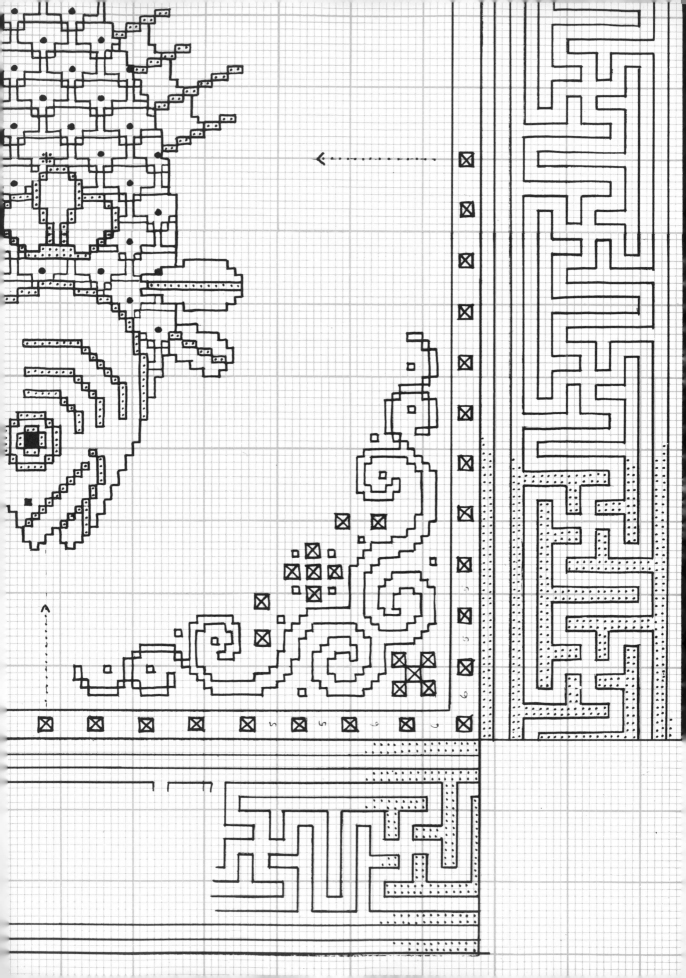

9. Using #1 tone outline and fill in upper and lower fins.

10. Using #4 tone work 3 areas marked in black at root of tail.

11. Using #2 tone work 4 dotted or shaded areas at root of tail.

12. Using #1 tone outline, then fill in tail.

13. Using #5 tone work Smyrna cross-stitch dots in band around field. NOTE: For the most part, 5 stitches separate dot from dot. However, at the corners 6 stitches separate the corner dot from the next dot, on upper and lower band. And on the side bands the upper and lower corner dots are separated by 6 stitches from the first dot, and 6 stitches separate the first dot from the second. So count carefully.

14. Using #1 tone work background of dotted band.

15. Work corner motifs using #1 tone for the scrolled pattern and #2 tone for the floating dots and Smyrna cross-stitches.

16. Using #5 tone work background of face of pillow.

FLAPS

17. Using #2 tone work bands above and below swastika motif. NOTE: Work upper and lower flaps with stitches slanting in the same direction as stitches on face of pillow. Work side flaps so stitches slant at right angles to stitches on face of pillow.

18. Using #1 tone work swastika motif on flaps.

19. Using #5 tone work background of flaps, shaded area on graph.

Bumblebee Pillow, Boxed · 12" x 16" x 2½"

The face of the canvas measures 141 threads by 191 threads. The flaps are 31 stitches deep. Bind off a piece of #12 canvas measuring 21" x 25". Then mark your outlines including those for the flaps. Mark the center threads and graph lines in the area on the surface of the pillow where you will work the bumblebee.

The following tones and colors are suggested for the bumblebee pillow:

1. Light   Off-White
2. Medium light   Putty
3. Medium   Gold
4. Medium dark   Olive Brown
5. Dark   Black

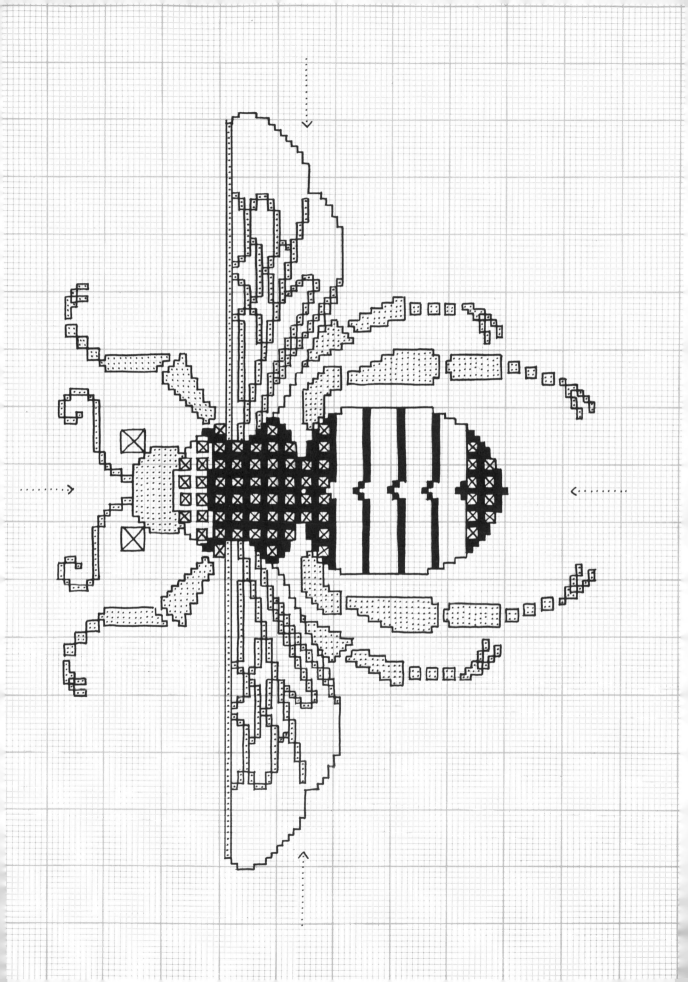

NOTE: There is a white dot in the middle of the bee's waist. It represents the intersection of the center threads of the canvas. Use it for reference when you begin work.

1. Using #4 tone work the dark parts of the bee's body. These are black on the graph. The small squares appearing in these two areas have, however, been left white in order that the symbol for the Smyrna cross-stitch will be obvious. First

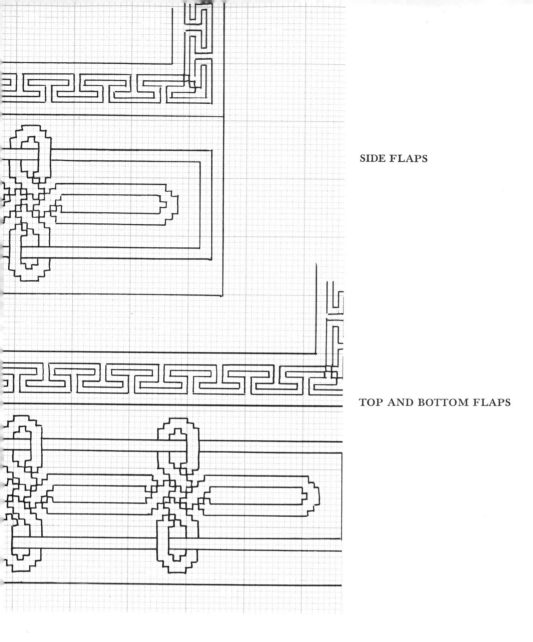

work the Smyrna cross-stitches, then fill in the rest of the dark areas, including the stripes. Then work the head and the antennae, or feelers.

2. Using #3 tone work Smyrna cross-stitches behind bee's head. Then fill in background in this area. Work light areas between stripes on bee's body. Work double Leviathan stitches for eyes.

3. Using #2 tone work the veins in the wings.

4. Using #1 tone work the wings. I find it best to outline, then fill in.

5. Using #4 tone work the 6 legs.

6. Using #5 tone work key fret around edge of face of pillow.

7. Using #1 tone work background of key fret border.

8. Using #5 tone fill in background of face of pillow.

9. Using #1 tone work white band and broken X on each flap. NOTE: Work top and bottom flaps with stitches slanting in same direction as stitches on face of pillow. Work side flaps with stitches slanting at right angles to stitches on face of pillow.

10. Using #3 tone work "frog" pattern, or the knot and bow design on the flaps.

11. Using #5 tone work background of flaps.

NOTE:　Below is a graphed diamond-shaped area for initials. Use it on the bottom flap in place of the center knot if you wish to sign your work.

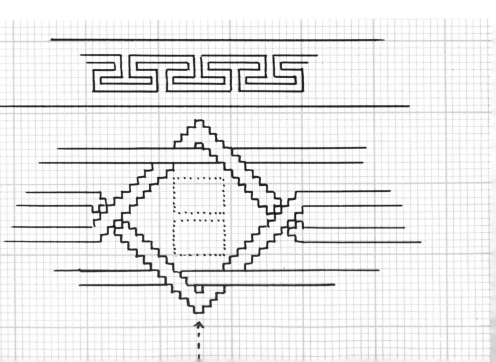

Frog Pillow · 17 ½″ x 17 ½″

The frog pillow measures 207 threads by 207 threads. Bind off a piece of #12 canvas measuring 22″ square. Mark the outlines, the center threads, and the graph lines where you will work the frog.

The following tones are suggested for the frog:

1. Pure white
2. Off-white
3. Light neutral
4. Medium tone. Accent color
5. Medium dark tone. Background color
6. Dark tone, like navy or black

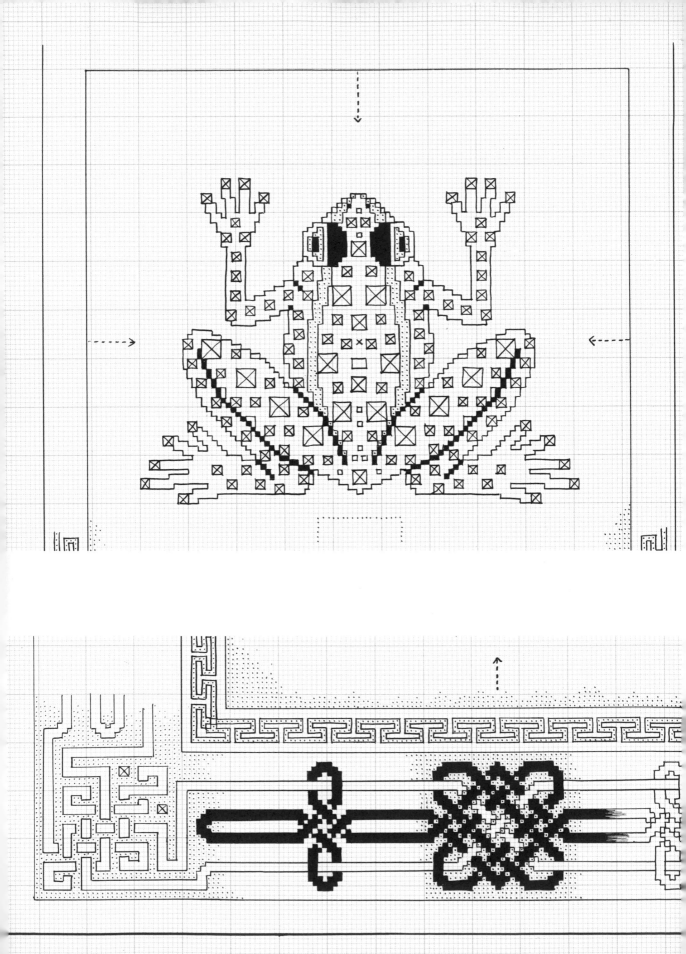

Note: On the graph an X in the center of the frog's back represents the intersection of the center threads of the canvas. Use it for reference when you begin work.

1. Using #3 tone work eyelids and outline lines within body, those at shoulders, and outlining legs. They are marked in black on the graph.

2. Using #1 tone work stripes on frog's body. They are dotted or shaded on the graph and run from the lower part of the frog's body up to the tip of his nose.

3. Using #4 tone, the accent color, work lumps on frog.

4. Using #1 tone work white outline around iris and pupil area of eyes. Work #4 tone, accent color, iris and #6 tone, black pupil in each eye. Work #6 tone nostril.

5. Using #2 tone outline frog's body, then fill in.

6. Using #1 tone work Smyrna cross-stitches for finger and toenails.

7. Using #5 tone, background color, work key fret.

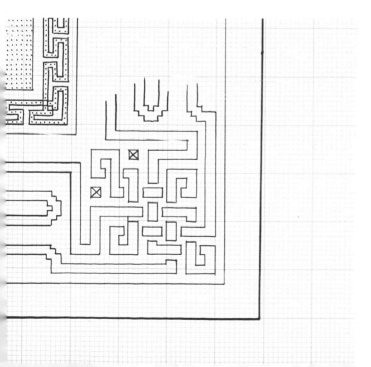

8. Using #2 tone work background of key fret.

9. Using #5 tone fill in background within border.

10. Using #2 tone work corner motifs and broken x bands in outer border.

11. Using #4 tone work 2 lumps in each corner motif.

12. Using #4 tone work "frog" knots and bows in border. They are marked in black on the graph.

13. Using #5 tone work background of outer border.

14. Using #2 tone work 7-row band at outer edge of pillow.

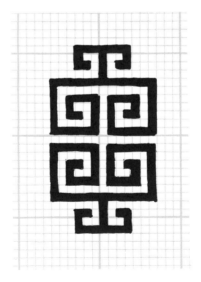

A small motif which can be used alone or in combination with others

Crab Pillow, Boxed · 12 x" 12" x 2½"

The face of the pillow measures 147 threads by 147 threads. The flaps are 29 threads deep. Bind off a piece of #12 canvas measuring 21" x 21". Mark your outlines, including those for the flaps. Mark center threads. In the center of the canvas mark the graph lines where you will work the crab.

The following tones are suggested for the crab pillow:
1. Lightest tone, white
2. Light tone, light neutral
3. Medium tone, accent color
4. Darkest tone, background color

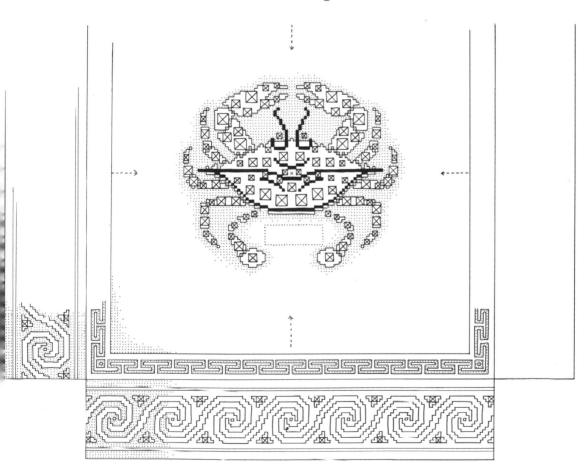

An **X** in the middle of the crab's shell marks the center of the graph and represents the intersection of the center threads of the canvas. Use it for reference when you begin work.

1. Using #2 tone work lines marked in black on crab's shell. Work Smyrna cross-stitches for eyes.

2. Using #3 tone work lumps in crab's shell.

3. Using #1 tone outline shell, then fill it in.

4. Using #1 tone work lumps on legs and claws, then fill in each segment of each leg and claw.

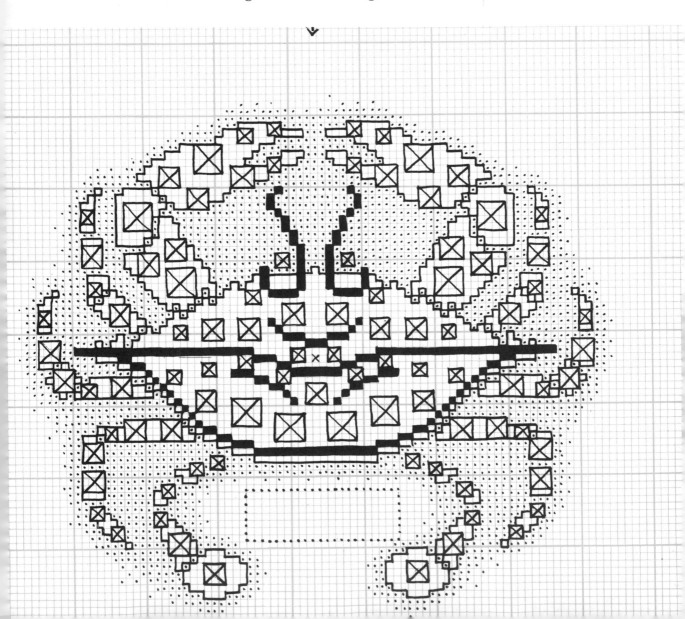

5. Using #2 tone work initials. The space is very empty if you do not decorate it.

6. Using #4 tone work key fret.

7. Using #1 tone work background of key fret.

8. Using #4 tone work background of face of pillow.

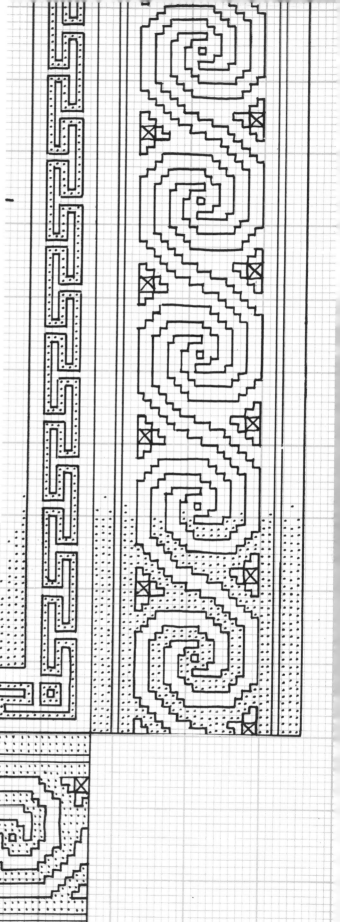

9. Using #2 tone work inner and outer single lines on flaps. NOTE: Work upper and lower flaps with stitches slanted in same direction as stitches on face of pillow: Work side flaps with stitches slanted at right angles to stitches on face of pillow.

10. Using #3 tone work small triangles on flaps. They are above and below the connection between each S-scroll. Then work Smyrna cross-stitch in each triangle.

11. Using #1 tone work interlocking S-scrolls on flaps. See diagram for easy break-up of scroll design, which is all one color.

    a. Work stitches shown in black.
    b. Work dotted stitches.
    c. Work stitches shown in white.

12. Using #4 tone work background of flaps.

A rug, 4½x6½; the straight lines of the border contrast with the curves of the dragon and waves.

A belt made in the Braid Pattern diagrammed on page 107.

The crab on this pillow is the one shown on page 63
but combined with the border on page 83.

Fish pillow, as shown on page 49.

Directions for the Lion on page 90, the border on page 48.

To make the Turtle pillow, see page 41.

Directions for the Circular Floral pillow and its boxing start on page 72.

Bumblebee pillow, as shown on page 54.

Butterfly Pillow, Boxed ·
12 x" 16" x 2½"

The face of the canvas measures 141 threads by 191 threads. The flaps are 31 stitches deep. Bind off a piece of #12 canvas measuring 21" x 25". Mark your outlines including those for the flaps. Mark center threads. Then mark the graph lines in the area on the surface of the pillow where you will work the butterfly.

The following 7 tones and colors are suggested for the butterfly pillow:

1. Light — Off-White
2. Medium light — Putty
3. Medium — Gold
4. Medium — Burnt-Orange
5. Medium dark — Olive Brown
6. Dark — Royal Navy
7. Dark — Black

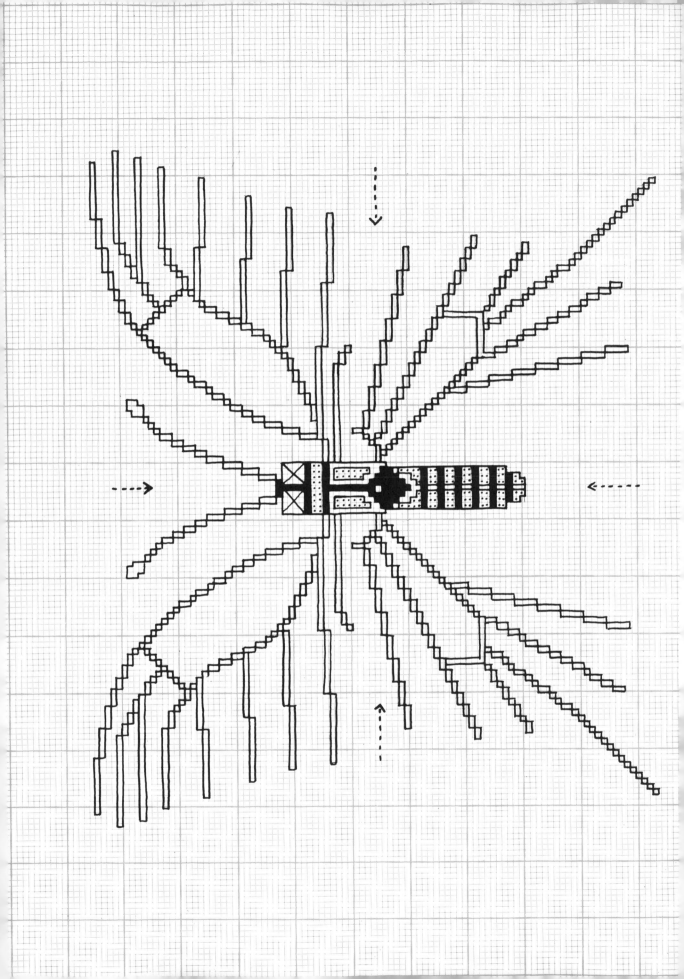

NOTE: On the graph a white dot in the upper part of the diamond on the body of the butterfly represents the intersection of the center threads on the canvas. Use it for reference when you begin work.

1.   Using #6 tone work black lines and diamond in butterfly's body.

2.   Using #3 tone work light lines in body.

3.   Using #5 tone work dotted or shaded areas in body.

4.   Using full strand of #4 tone work double Leviathan stitches for eyes.

5.   Using #3 tone work antennae, or feelers.

6.   Using #2 tone work veins in butterfly's wings.

This graph shows only the body and wings, to make starting the design easier. The full design is shown on the next two pages.

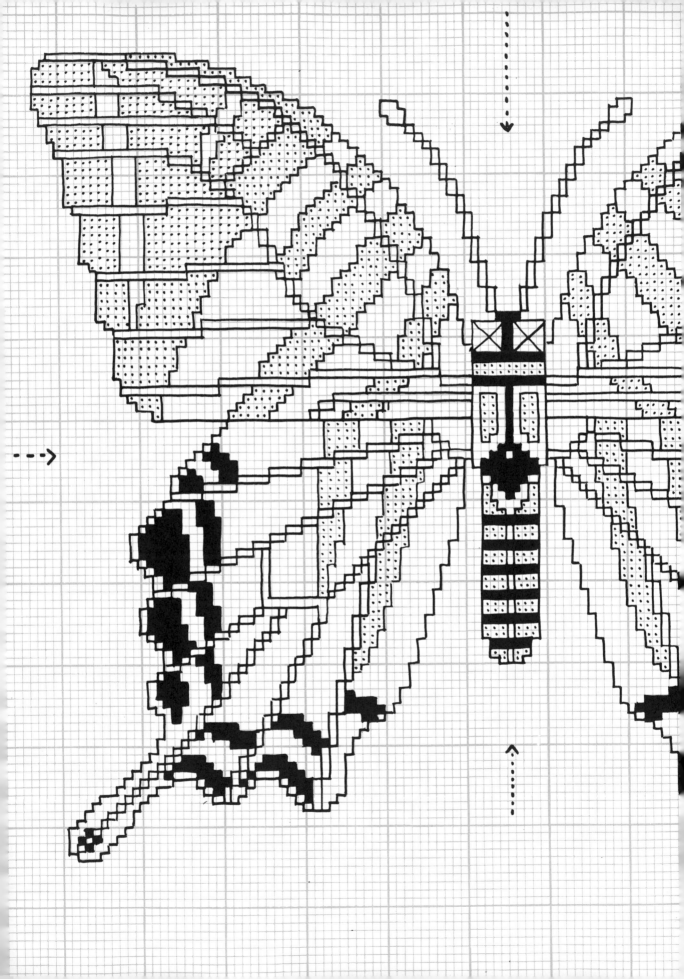

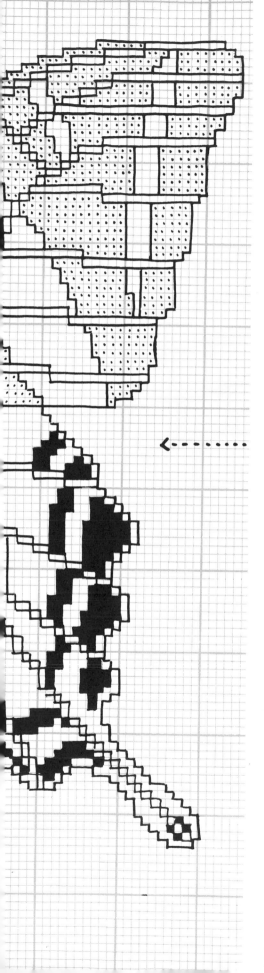

7. Using #3 tone work white areas in tips of upper wings. Then work areas at roots of wings as shown in illustration.

8. Using #5 tone work shaded or dotted areas in upper and lower wings.

9. Using #6 tone work black pattern at edges of lower wings.

10. Using #1 tone work the white areas of the wings.

11. Using #7 tone work key fret pattern of border. I work it in three steps: See illustration.

   a. Work stitches shown in black.

   b. Work stitches shown in white.

   c. Work row of dotted stitches.

12. Using #1 tone work background of key-fret.

13. Using #7 tone fill in background of face of pillow.

14. Work flaps as indicated in directions for bumblebee.

Circular Floral Pillow, Boxed · 11" diameter, 2½" boxing

Bind off 2 pieces of #12 canvas, one 15" square for the face of the pillow, and one 40" x 6" for the boxing. Mark the center lines and the graph lines on the square piece. Do not try to mark the outline of the circle. You will do this by counting when you work the outer border in wool.

Count off and outline 385 threads for the length of the boxing, and 31 threads for the width if you plan to work the butterfly band, or 27 threads for the width if you plan to work the fluttering ribbon band.

An X at the top of the fretwork vase marks the center of the graph. It corresponds to the crossing of the two center

threads on your canvas. Use this mark as a point of reference when you begin work.

Five tones and colors are suggested for the floral pillow:

1.	Light	Off-White
2.	Medium light	Pale Blue
3.	Medium	Blue
4.	Medium dark	Deep Blue
5.	Dark	Navy

1. Using #3 tone work the fretwork vase, including the tassels and handle, i.e., that part of the vase marked in black on the graph.

2. Using #2 tone work the dotted or shaded portion of the vase, including the tassels.

3. Using #1 and #3 tone work flower in the square in the middle of the fat part of the vase, then fill in the background of the square with #2.

4. Using #3 tone work all the flower stems except the two marked in black on the graph. Work these either in #2 or #4 tone. Work the leaves in light and dark, #2 and #4.

5. Work the flowers. The two large ones at the top should be worked in the following manner: #4 where it is shown in black on the graph, #3 where it is shown dotted or shaded, #2 for the white petals, and #1 for the center, with #5 for the dots.

6. The downward-facing flowers at the ends of the 2 arched stems, black stems on the graph, should be done as follows:

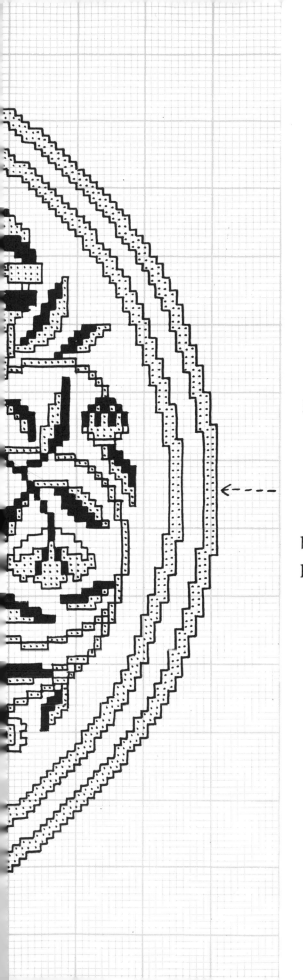

#4 tone for the black lines,
#3 tone for the dotted or
shaded portions, and #2
tone for the upper sides of
the flowers.

7. Work all the other flowers.

8. Using #1 tone work 2 dotted bands around the face
   of the pillow.

9. Using #2 tone work band
   between two shaded bands.

10. Using #5 tone work back-
    ground of face of pillow.

Two alternate designs for the
box banding are shown on
pages 76 and 77.

Butterfly Banding

1. Using #1 tone work outline of each panel.

2. Using #1 and #3 tone work body and antennae, or feelers of butterflies, #3 tone for shaded lines, #1 tone for white. #1 tone for eyes, black dots on graph.

3. Upper wings of butterfly shade from #1 in areas next to the body, through #2 and #3, to #4 at tips of wings, with two #1 dots. Under wings of butterfly shade from #2 tone next to the body out to #4 tone at tips of wings, with two #1 dots.

4. Using #5 tone fill in background inside panels.

5. Using #2 tone work background of boxing strip.

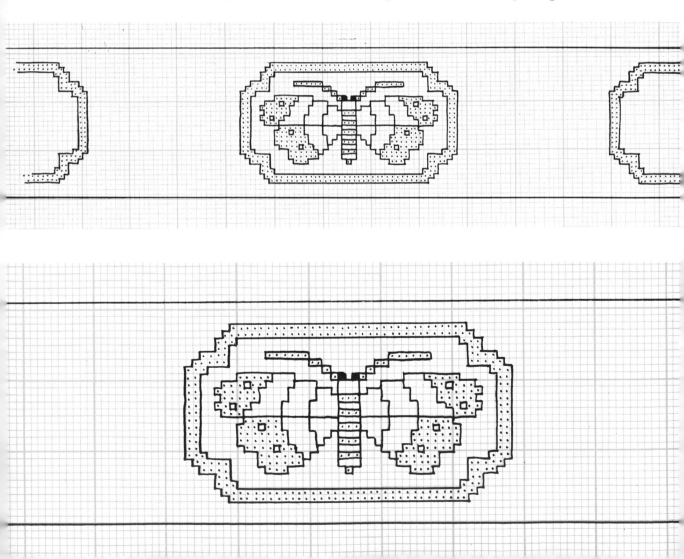

Fluttering Ribbon Banding

1. Using #5 tone for white part of ribbons and #1 tone for dotted or shaded areas on graph, work fluttering ribbon motifs.

2. Using #2 tone work background of boxing strip.

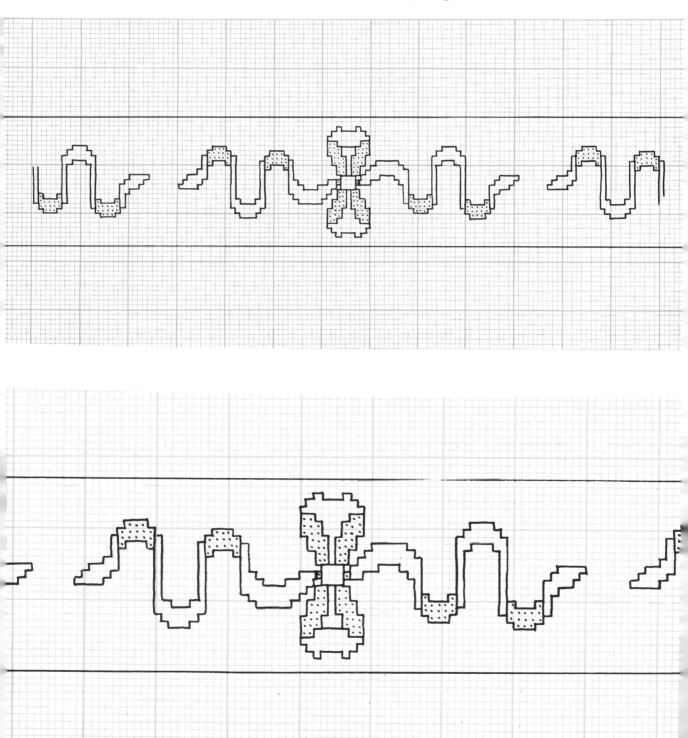

A scenic design worked in five shades of blue and an off-white

Serenity Pillow · 16" x 16"

The pillow measures 192 threads x 192 threads. Bind off a piece of #12 canvas measuring 20" x 20". Mark the center lines and the outlines. Then mark the graph lines in the center where you will work the octagon motif. (The central design is a combination of the 8 trigrams, from the "I Ching," and a stylized version of a Chinese character for happiness.)

Three tones are used in the serenity pillow:

1. Light
2. Medium
3. Dark

Many handsome combinations of colors are possible here: White, gray and black: gray-white, cognac and eggplant: White, bitter green and navy: white, saffron yellow and burnt-orange, etc.

TOP

✛ marks the center of the graph and corresponds to the crossing of the center lines on the canvas.

1. Using #1 tone work the character in the center of the octagon motif. Work the outline around it. This line circles the shaded, or dotted area, the background for the character. Work the outline of the octagon, then the eight trigrams.

2. Using #3 tone fill in shaded area around central character.

3. Using #2 tone fill in background behind eight trigrams, (the background in the octagon collar around the central character).

4. Using #1 tone work outline around field. This is the band, two stitches wide, with in-turning corners. (See next page.)

5. Using #2 tone work Smyrna cross-stitches in the field, within the area just outlined.

6. With #1 tone work inner and outer bands outlining swastika border.

7. With #3 tone work Smyrna cross-stitches in area between band worked in step 4 and the inner band of the swastika border. These stitches are represented, on the graph, by shaded, or dotted squares. And at each corner there is a large square, a double Leviathan stitch, surrounded by four Smyrna cross-stitches.

8. Using #3 tone fill in field.

9. Using #2 tone fill in area directly outside the in-turning outline of the field. In step 7 you worked the bumps in this band.

10. Using #1 tone work swastikas.

11. Using #3 tone work background of swastika border, dotted, or shaded, on the graph.

12. Using #2 tone work outer border of pillow, the band 7 stitches deep.

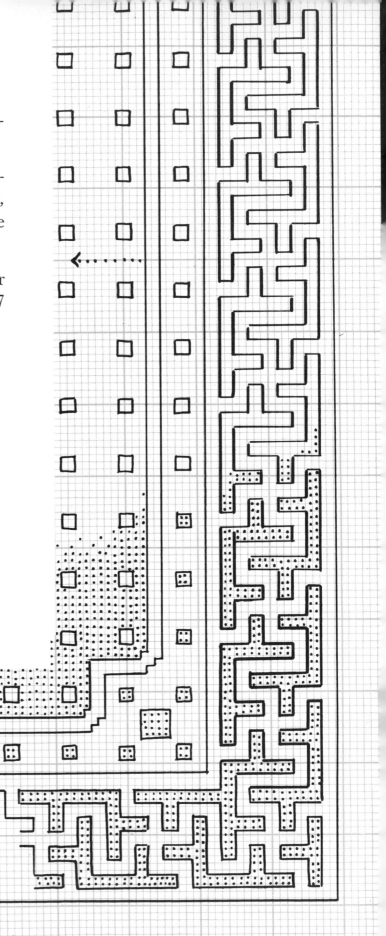

Double Dragon Pillow · 16" x 16"

Double Dragon Pillow · 16" x 16"

The pillow measures 191 threads by 191 threads. Bind off a piece of #12 canvas measuring 20" x 20". Mark the center threads, then outline the pillow. Mark the graph lines where you will work the double dragon motif in the center of the pillow.

Only two tones are used in this design.
1. Light
2. Dark

NOTE: You can also work it in reverse, dark pattern against light ground.

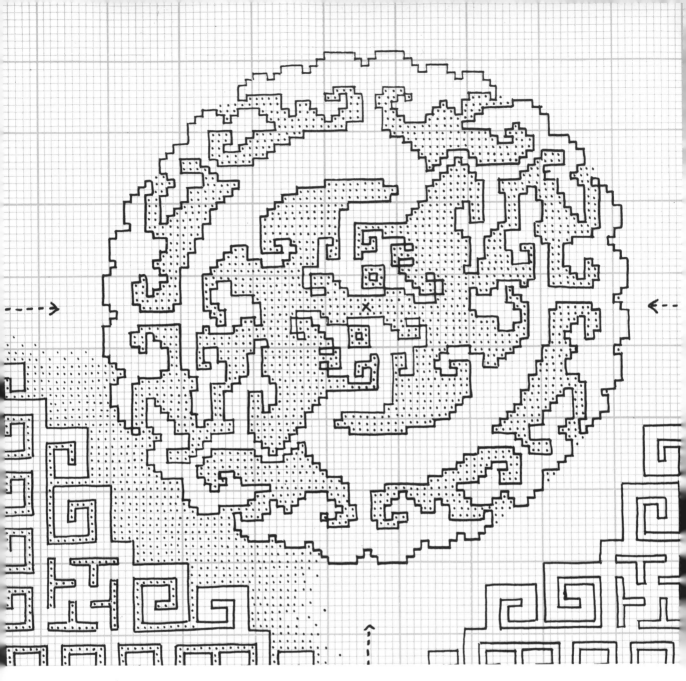

An X, between the dragons' heads, marks the center of the graph and represents the intersection of the center threads on your canvas.

Using #1 tone for all the pattern areas:

1. Work double dragon motif.

2. Work outlines of dotted border, then dots, counting carefully, because at the centers and the corners the count changes from 7 stitches between dots to 6 stitches between dots.

3.   Work frets in corners within dotted band.

4.   Work inner and outer band of swastika border. Then work swastikas.

5.   Using #2 tone work background of pillow, including band, two stitches wide, outside swastika border.

6.   Using #1 tone, work outer band, 7 stitches deep.

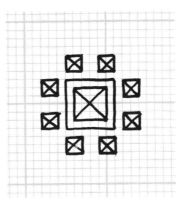

A small motif which can be used alone or in combination with others

Mouse Eating Apricots

When working the leaves on the mouse pillow work the pale center vein first, then outline each leaf with the same pale tone. After this, work from outside of leaf toward center. Work a single row slightly darker than outline tone, then another slightly darker, until you have filled in leaf, with darkest tone along the central vein. Work under sides of leaves with the medium tone.

Work apricots with darkest tone at outer edge. Use a shade lighter for each of the two outlined rows until you reach the body of the fruit, to be worked in the lightest of the four tones of apricot.

Use a medium tone of apricot for the initials and the rounded rectangle around them.

Work the border in a medium tone.

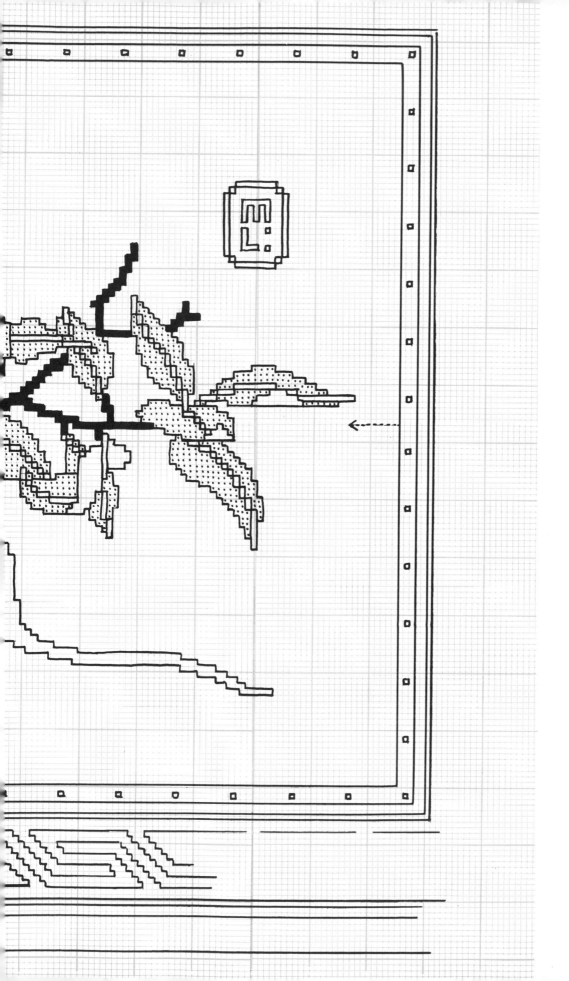

Lion Pillow, Boxed · 8″ x 12″ x 2⅛″

The face of the pillow measures 96 threads by 144 threads. The flaps are 26 threads deep. Bind off a piece of #12 canvas measuring 16″ x 20″. Mark center lines. Mark the outlines, including those for the flaps. Then mark the graph lines in the area in the middle of the canvas where you will work the lion.

The following tones and colors are suggested for the lion pillow:

1.	Light	Bone
2.	Medium light	Beige or Fawn
3.	Medium dark	Taupe
4.	Dark	Black or Brown

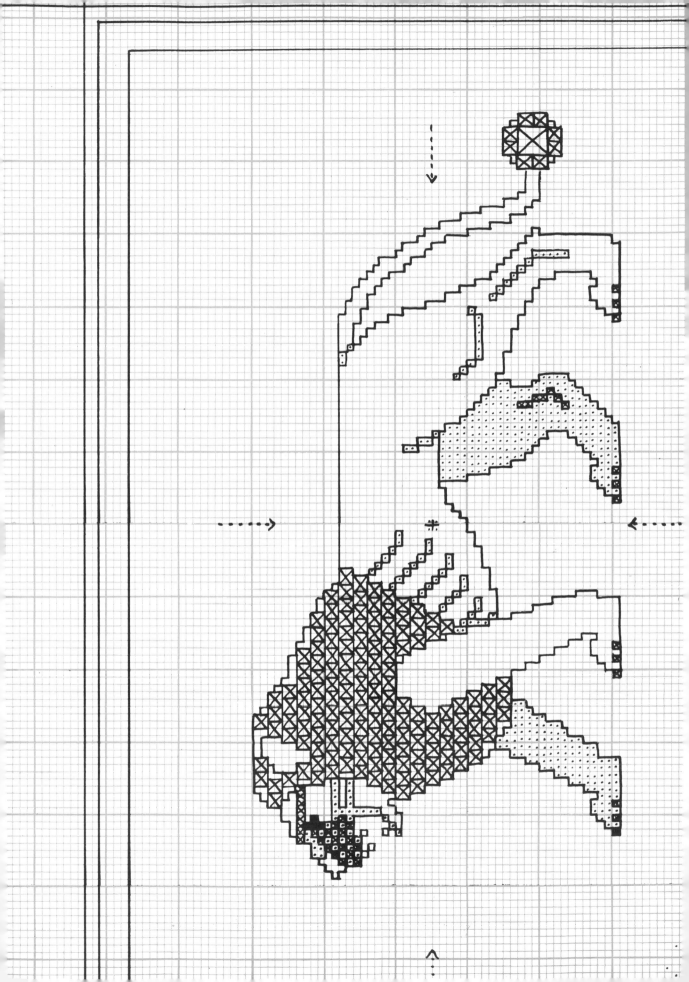

✛ marks the center of the graph and indicates the center of the canvas. Use this point for reference when you begin work.

1. Using #2 tone work the dotted squares in the lions's face.

2. Using #3 tone work the X'd squares in the lion's face.

3. Using #4 tone work lion's eye.

4. Using #1 tone work white stitches in lion's head, including teeth and ears.

5. Using #3 tone work lion's mane in Smyrna cross-stitch. Also use #3 tone for the regular stitches appearing at the upper and lower edges of the mane area.

6. Using #2 tone work lines for lion's ribs, and for the muscle lines in the hind leg nearest tail. Also work the lines separating that leg from the body. Work the lines separating the front leg from the body. Work the three stitches separating the tail from the body.

7. Using #1 tone outline lion's body, two unshaded legs, and tail, up to the tuft. Then fill in outlined area with #1 tone.

8. Using #3 tone work tuft at end of tail: Double Leviathan Stitch surrounded by eight Smyrna cross-stitches. Work muscle line in shaded hind leg, and toe-nails in each foot.

9. Using #2 tone outline, then fill in, the two shaded legs.

10. Using #4 tone work Smyrna cross-stitches in band at edge of face of pillow.

11. Using #1 tone work white background for this band.

12. Using #4 tone work background of pillow face, including narrow band, two threads wide, outside the dotted band.

13. Using #1 tone work fret borders and bands on flaps.

NOTE: Work upper and lower flaps with stitches slanting at the same angle as those on face of pillow. Work two side flaps with stitches slanting at right angles to stitches on face of pillow.

14. Using #4 tone work background to flaps.

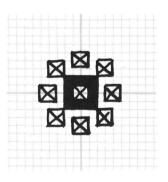

A small motif which can be used alone or in combination with ot

Covering A Parsons Table

The pattern for a Parsons table will cover a table measuring 15″ x 15″ x 17″ high. The work is done on #8 Penelope canvas. Most of the central motifs in the book can be used on the table top.

Have a carpenter make a table for you exactly to your specifications. Ask for a 2″ apron and 2″ square legs.

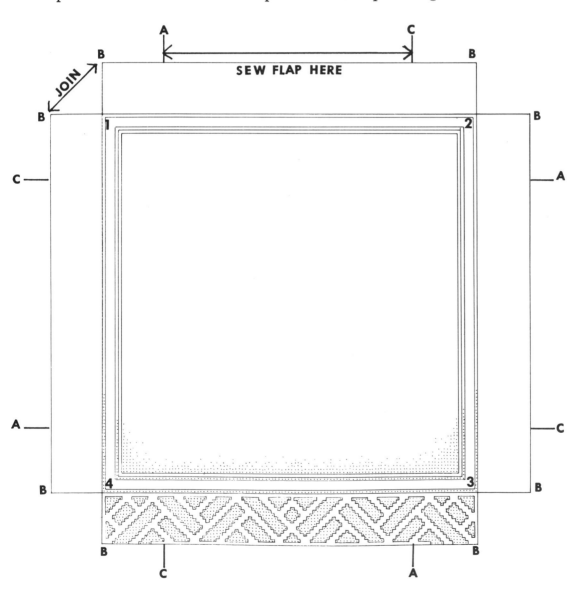

The top is made with four side flaps, each being 2″ deep. Four leg covers, 15″ high, must also be made. Each will be 8″ wide because each piece covers four sides of a leg, and each leg side measures 2″ in width.

Work the top rectangle. NOTE: Use four strands of yarn when working within the square on the top of the table, (but on the flaps and the legs use only three strands, the full thread). Cut one hank of yarn only once. Then take a long thread, peel away one strand, slip the remaining two strands through the eye of the needle, and pull the ends even. You now have four strands of thread without the bulk of 8 at the eye of the needle. This makes work easier because you now do not have to yank the needle through the canvas at each stitch. Before you begin working with the four strand thread, however, lock the thread directly behind the eye of the needle. You do this by turning the point of the needle back on the thread as close as possible to where the thread passes through the eye of the needle. Pierce the four strands with the point of the needle. Pull the needle through the wool and you have a kind of twisting of the thread a needle's length away from the eye. Your thread will now pull evenly rather than slipping at the eye of the needle.

When working the side flaps change the direction of your stitch. This will give a clean fold line where the flaps turn down to cover the aprons. In the same way alternate the direction of your stitch from panel to panel when you work the leg covers. Work two covers with stitch directions as follows: ↘↗ ↘↗ and two covers with stitch directions as follows: ↗↖ ↗↖ . When you sew the legs to the top you will understand the reason behind this peculiar instruction.

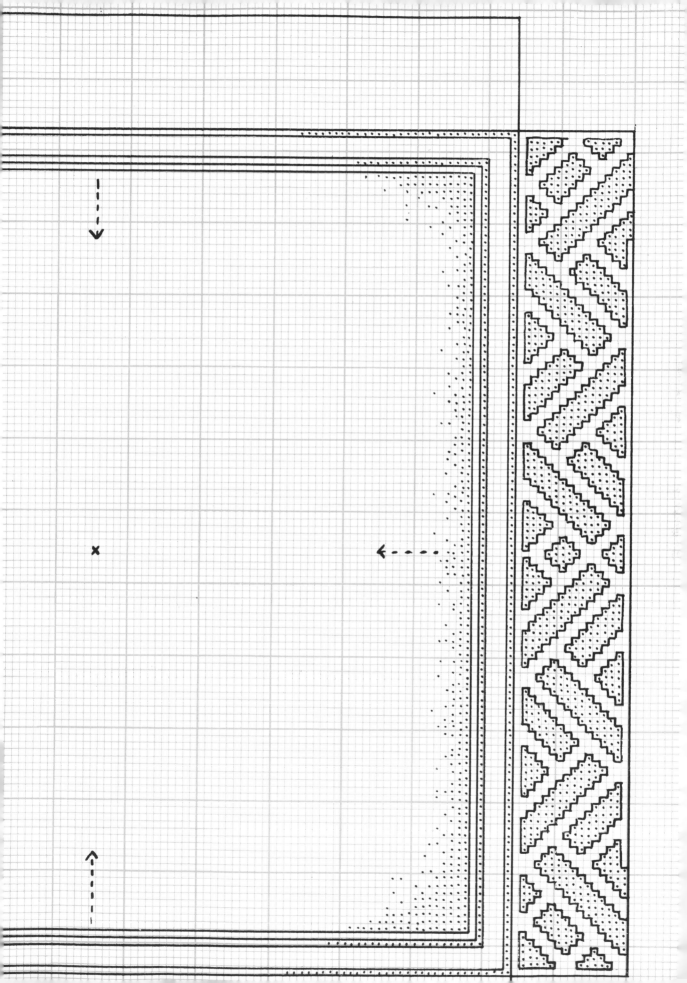

When you have finished all five pieces, block them. Then, with insides out, sew the corners of the table top. See diagram. Trim to within 8 double threads, or 1″ from seams. Then sew the four leg covers to the four corners of the top. Sew 16 stitches to either side of the corners of the top. See illustration. Sew the seams by hand, without catching in the seam allowance left at the corners. The five pieces of canvas will now look like a dog blanket with four open legs.

Next sew four canvas flaps, 3″ deep, to the table top between legs, as shown by diagrams. Then cut off excess canvas, leaving 8 double threads for seam allowance. The flaps should now measure about 2″ from seam to raw edge.

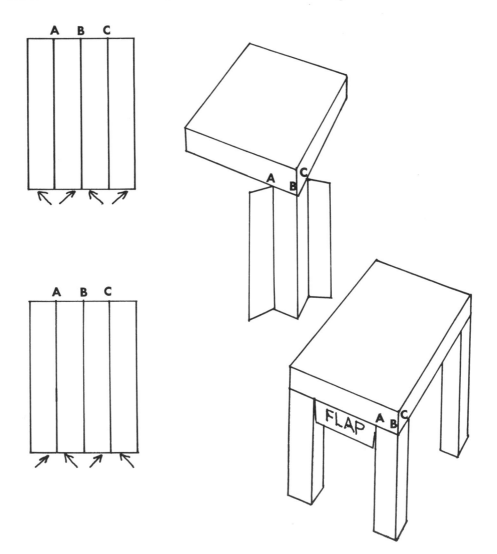

Work a row of needlepoint on the flaps. Do this on the first thread away from the seam. Work this row so the stitches slant in a direction opposite to the stitches on the apron.

Press all seams open. Place the cover on the table. Pull the top down so it fits snugly on the table. Use a staple gun to staple the top of the cover to the top of the table. Then staple the flaps to the under side of the table. Pull each flap until the apron of the table is completely covered by needlework, and the edge of the flap folds under along the under corner of the apron.

Clip off excess canvas on the sides of each leg, leaving 8 double threads, or 1″ seam allowance. Turn this under on each side of each leg. Wrap each leg in its cover and sew the seams along the inner corner of each leg. Do this by hand, using wool the color of the fretwork pattern. Sew through each meeting pair of holes in the canvas so the pattern joins and matches properly.

Turn under 1½″ excess at bottom of leg. Staple securely to bottom of leg.

Finish the table by sewing fabric lining to the under side of the table to cover staples and raw canvas. Do the same at the bottom of each leg. Then drive in four domes of silence, one in the center of the bottom of each leg, and you have completed the table.

Glasses Case

This graph is designed for #16 canvas. Bind off a piece of canvas measuring about 9″ x 12″. Count off the two work areas, side by side as shown. Then mark center threads and graph lines.

3 tones are used in this design.
1. Light
2. Medium
3. Dark

INTERTWINING KNOT SIDE

An X marks the center of the design and corresponds to the intersection of the center threads in the area outlined on your canvas. Use this mark as a point of reference when you begin work.

1. Using #1 tone work broken X band, shown in white on graph. (A pair of spectacles neatly tied in a complex black knot.) Then work white outline around the field of the case. A dotted band surrounds it, then the wide black border.

2. Using #3 tone work the knotted pattern shown in black on the graph.

3. Using #2 tone work background, dotted or shaded on graph, and the dotted outline inside black border.

4. Using #3 tone work outer border, black on graph.

ZIGZAG PATTERNED SIDE

1. Using #2 tone work dotted outline around center field of case. Here you may place your initials if you like.

2. Optional. Using #2 tone work initials.

3. Using #1 tone work white line around line worked in step 1.

4. Using #3 tone fill in central field. It was left white on the graph only so you could see the graph lines.

5. Using #1 tone outline zigzag area.

6. Using #2 tone work dotted outline next to outer black border.

7. Using #3 tone work outer border shown in black on the graph.

8. Using #1, #2, and #3 tones work zigzag pattern.

Beetle Glasses Case

This graph is designed for #18 canvas. Bind off a piece of canvas measuring about 9″ x 12″. Count off the two work areas side by side, as shown. Then mark graph lines within the two areas.

5 tones are used in this design:

1. Light
2. Medium light
3. Medium
4. Medium dark
5. Dark

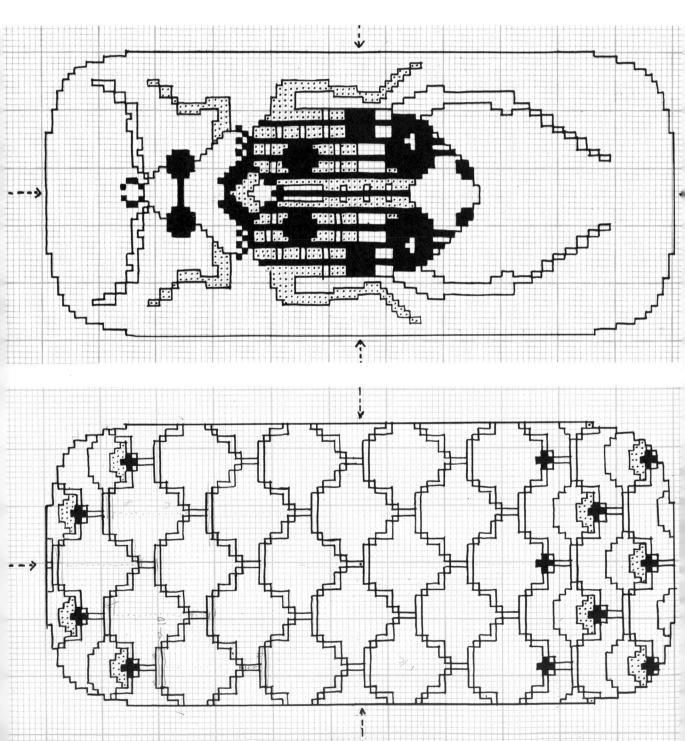

BEETLE SIDE

1. Using #5 tone work areas marked in black on the graph.

2. Using #1 tone work areas left white on beetle's back. Do not work the hind legs and head, shoulders and antennae, or feelers.

3. Using #3 tone work hind legs, head, shoulders and antennae, or feelers.

4. Using #4 tone work dotted or shaded areas on beetle's back, his forelegs and the legs behind the forelegs.

5. Using #2 tone fill in background. It helps to outline the curved ends before filling in the area.

SCALLOP-PATTERN SIDE

1. Using #1 tone outline scallops.

2. Using #5 tone work areas marked in black on graph. The pattern is an all-over repeat. I have left part of the graph only partially marked so you can read the scallop outline with ease.

3. Using #4 tone work dotted, or shaded crescents in each scallop.

4. Using #3 tone work next outlined crescent in each scallop.

5. Using #2 tone work balance of each scallop.

Needlebook

The needlebook design is to be worked in two tones. The area within the narrow border is for initials. They are to be worked in the lighter tone against the darker tone.

For the pattern begin work at the upper right-hand corner. Instructions for pattern:

1. Using tone #1 work single basket weave row from right to left. Then work from left to right using two continental stitches, side by side, every other row. Park your needle.

2. Using tone #2, going from left to right again, work two continental stitches, side by side, fitting them into those al-

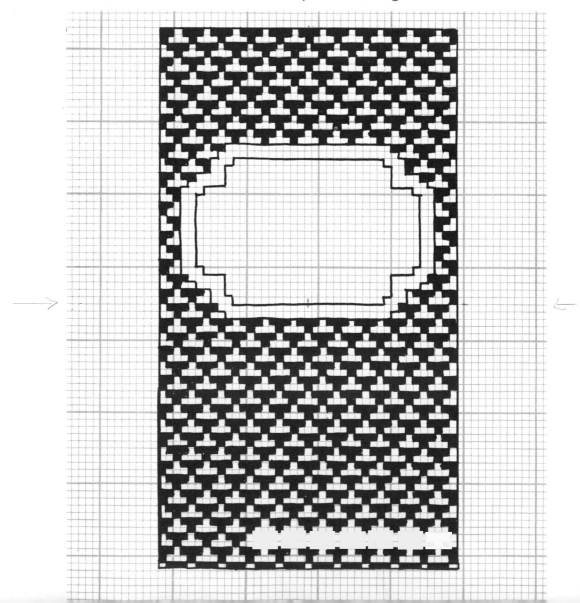

ready worked in tone #1. Then work a single row of basket weave from left to right. Park second needle.

3. Pick up needle used in step 1 and repeat step 1. Then repeat step 2. Continue in this way until you have covered the desired area with the all-over pattern.

Braid Pattern

The braid pattern is suitable for belts, suspenders, and luggage straps, and, when worked on a larger mesh, could be made into a bell-pull.

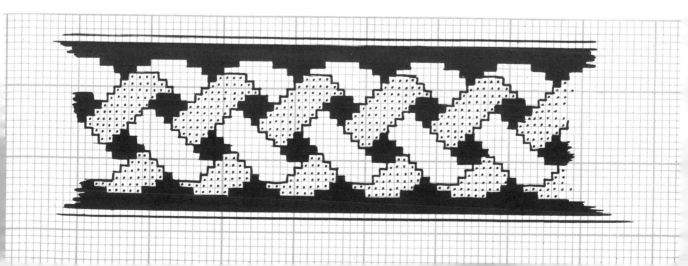

Scroll Pattern

This diagram shows how to turn the corner with the scroll pattern so you can use it for a flat border rather than a boxed border.

The all-over pattern in the field is worked at right angles to the direction in which you work the basketweave. The upper diagram on the next page shows how to work the light background, the lower, how to work the pattern.

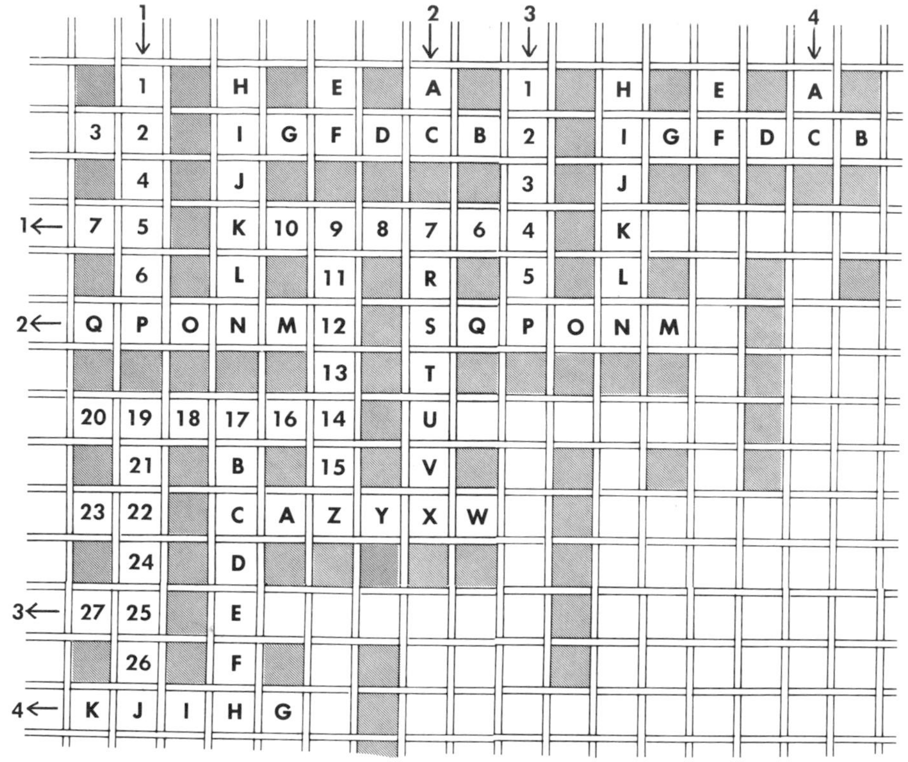

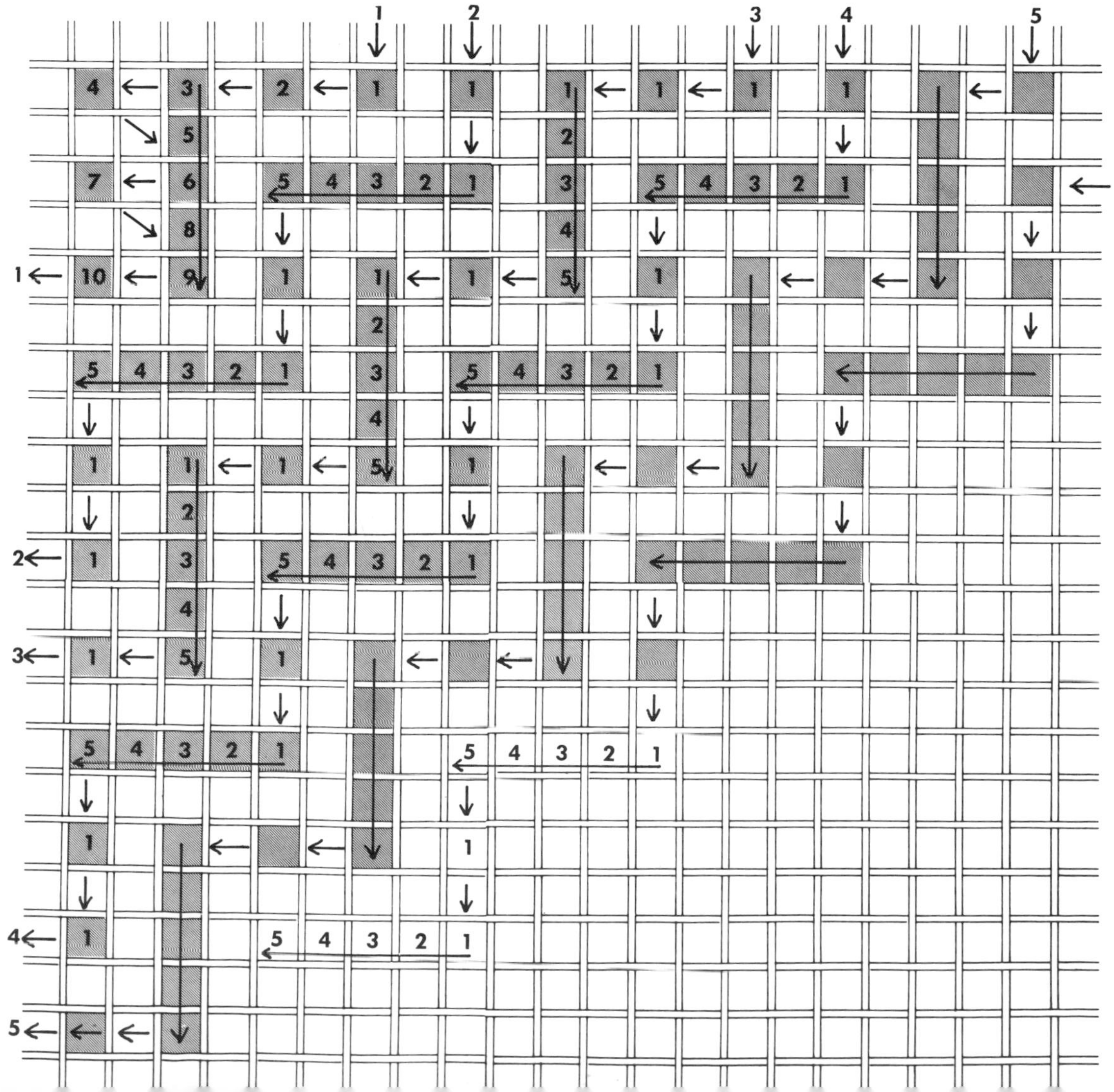

Alphabet

Here, in addition to the numerals from 1 to 0, is an alphabet of handsome letters. When used for names, dates, and short titles, these numbers and letters work up into attractive designs.

I suggest, however, that you first draw your idea on graph paper before working it out on canvas, for the simple reason that the spacing of letters is an art in itself. After you have copied the letters you need for your design, cut them out, separate them, and line them up on a fresh sheet of graph paper. Then move the letters about until they make a pleasant rhythm. On the chart, for example, you can see that the line containing the M, the N, and the O, looks dense. The spacing is too crowded when compared with the spacing of the letters in the other lines. So you should arrange your letters until the spacing is pleasing to your eye. Then glue each letter down on the graph paper, and proceed with your design. (Use rubber cement. It allows for easy re-arrangement of the letters if you have second thoughts about the spacing.)

I find that the border, shown in the illustration, is a comfortable one for the letters, it being made up of the band used for the uprights of most of the letters.

You have many designs to choose from for the boxed border. I used the scroll wave for "The Golden Dolphin," as appropriate for the aquatic nature of the title (page 114).

Just remember, figure the number of repeats you will use on your boxing before you outline the face of the pillow. The border band is flexible in terms of count, whereas the count required for the repeats on the boxing is not flexible.

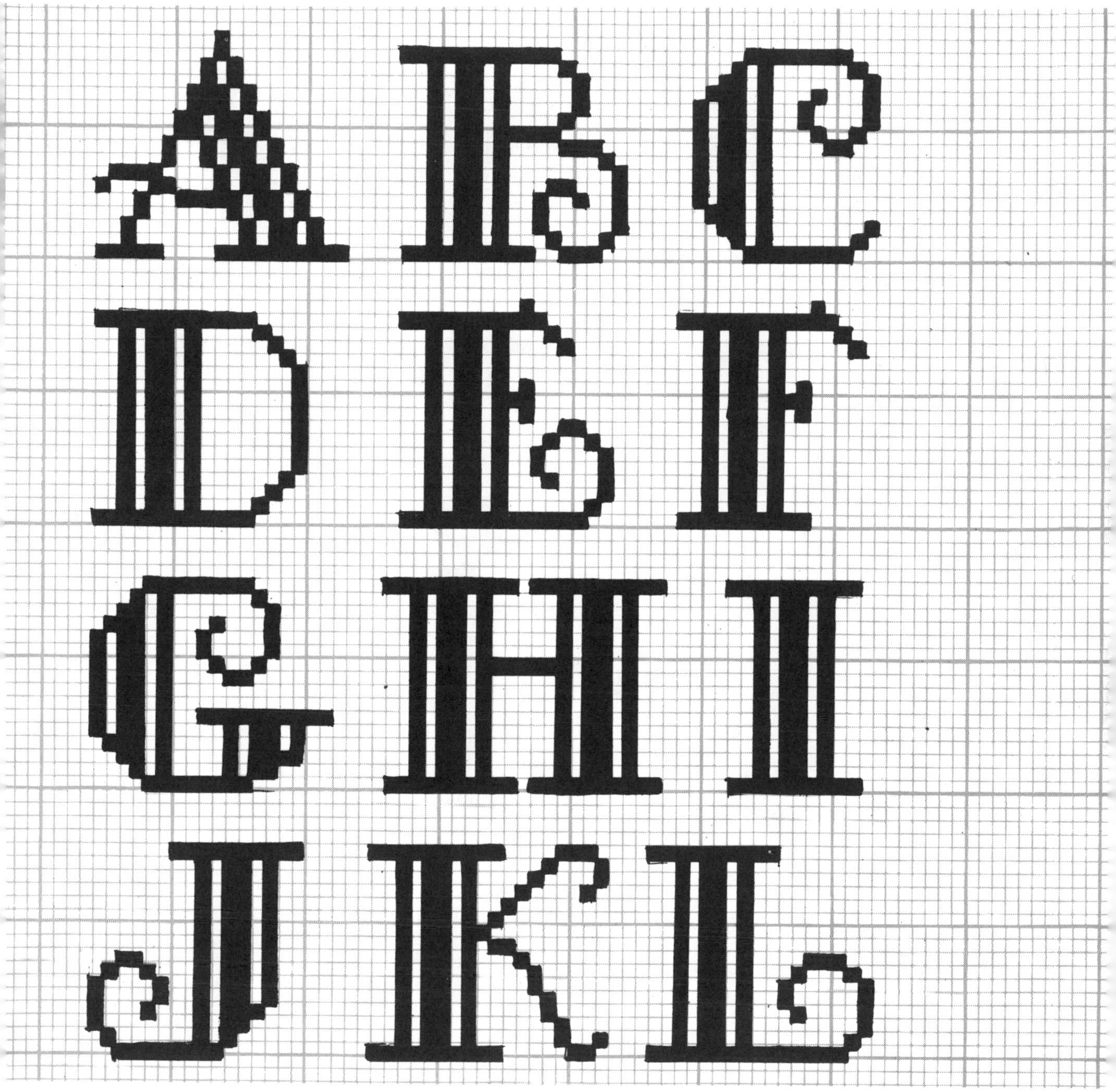

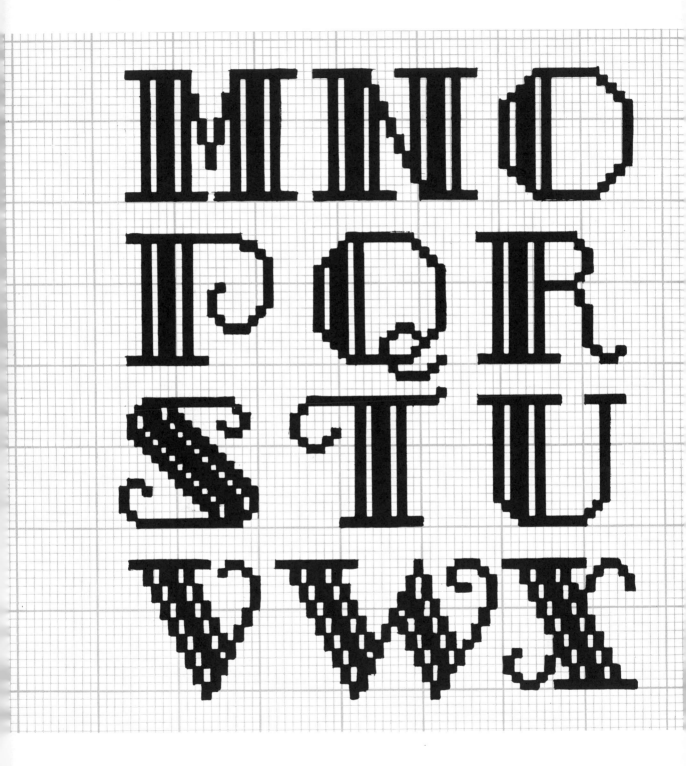

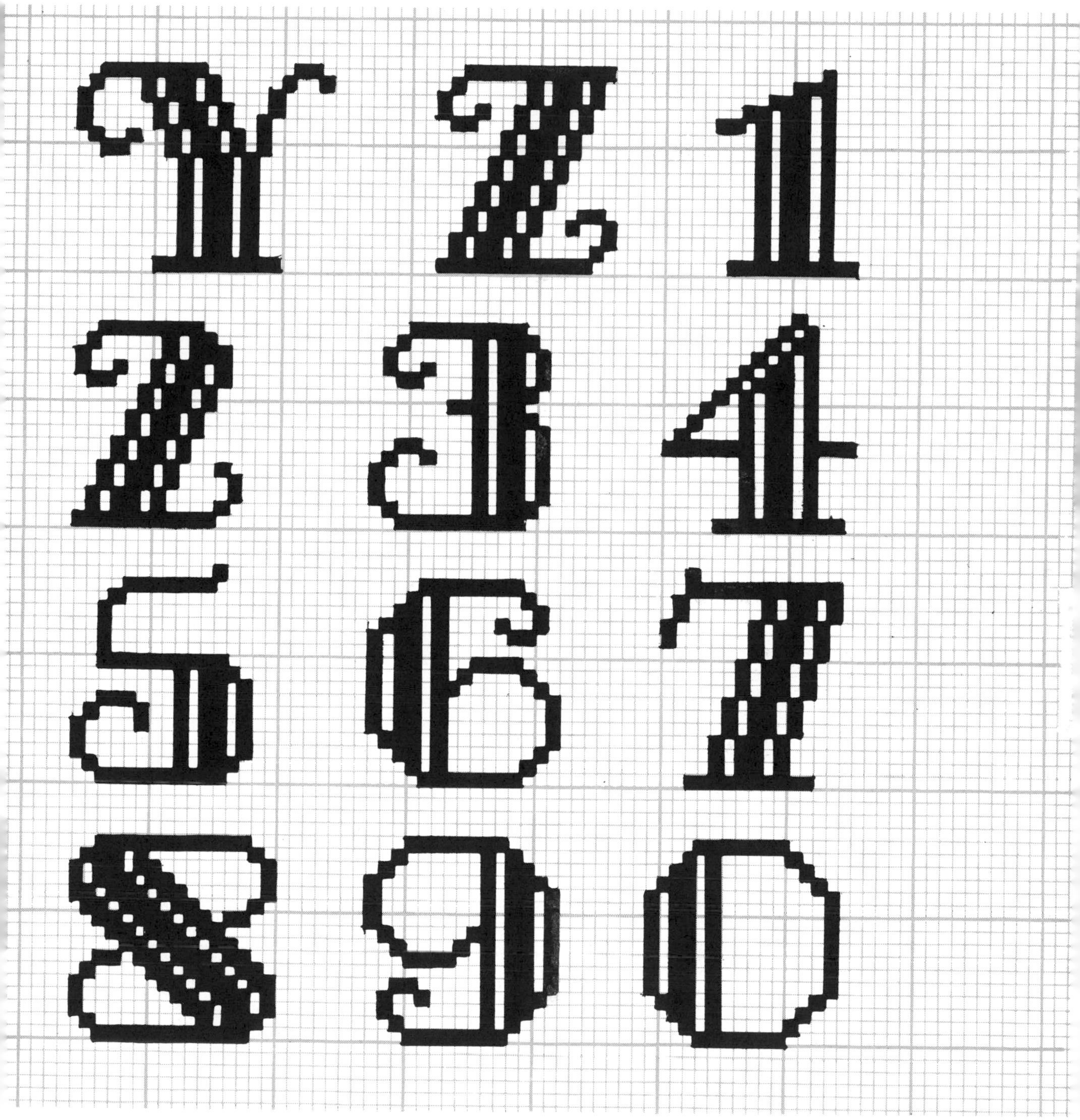

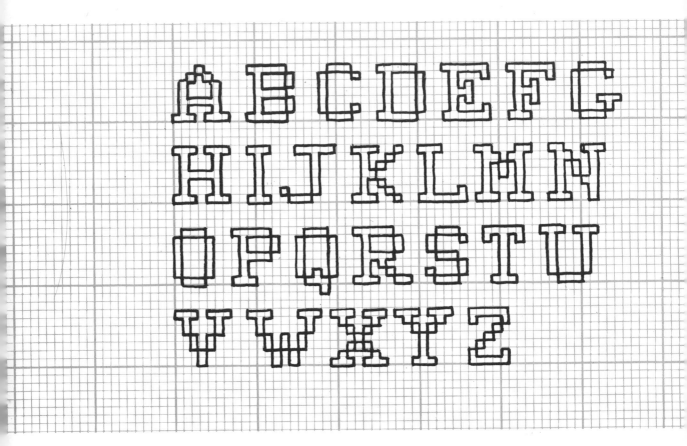